AUGMENTED CITY

A PARADIGM SHIFT

MAURIZIO CARTA

0 THE AUGMENTED CITY PARADIGM 04

Ten challenges for reimagining cities and communities

1 SENTIENT 18

The Sense/Active City: knowledge/solving urbanism for collaborative cities

2 OPENSOURCE 36

The Crowdsourcing Urbanism: the civic-tech-urban alliance in the sharing society

3 INTELLIGENT 58

The Intelligence of City: smart planning protocol for multilevel urban tools

4 PRODUCTIVE 86

The Fab City: creative / productive urban ecosystem

5 CREATIVE 104

The Creative Land: human creativity for active cities

6 RECYCLICAL — 132

The Re-cyclical Urbanism: a paradigm shift for the circular metamorphosis

7 RESILIENT — 160

The Proactive Ecology: resilient, circular and self-sufficient cities

8 FLUID — 198

The Fluid City: porosity and fluidity as projective paradigms

9 RETICULAR — 214

The Transconnected Society: metropolitan super-organism and territorial archipelagos

10 STRATEGIC — 232

The Hyper-Strategic Planning: incremental and adaptive planning processes

TEN CHALLENGES

THE AUGMENTED CITY PARADIGM
Ten challenges for reimagining cities and communities

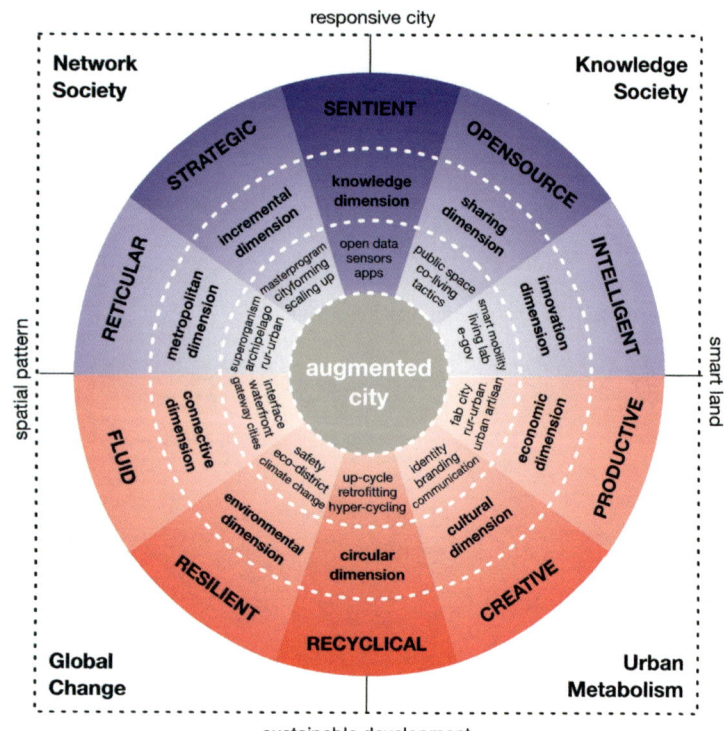

THE AUGMENTED CITY: URBANISM IN THE NEO-ANTHROPOCENE

By 2050, the world's urban population is expected to nearly double, making urbanisation one of the twenty-first century's most transformative trends and asking urbanism to give more innovative and effective solutions. Local populations and migrants, social and cultural interactions, environmental impacts and economic activities are increasingly concentrated in cities, and this poses massive sustainability challenges in terms of reimagining how to plan and manage housing, infrastructures, basic services, food security, health, education, decent jobs, safety and natural resources, among others. But, as affirmed in 2016 Quito Conference "UN Habitat III", we are still far from adequately addressing these and other existing and emerging challenges, and the **New Urban Agenda** (UN, 2017) asks to take advantage of the opportunities presented by urbanism as an engine/tool of sustainable and inclusive economic growth, social innovation, cultural development, environmental protection, and of its contributions to the achievement of creative, intelligent, safe and resilient urban development. To fully harness the innovative and creative potential of cities (metropolitan or rural, dense or sprawled, traditional or new), we need an **urban paradigm shift** grounded in integrated and indivisible dimensions of sustainable development: environmental, cultural, social, territorial and economic.

The future of urbanism – as technical discipline and form of human habitat both – needs a disruptive renewal of paradigms, a frantic whirlwind of experimentations and a continuous review of ingrained habits. In last decades the most conformist urbanism – with few unheeded critics – was too busy pouring concrete, increasing greenhouse gases emissions and consuming natural and cultural resources to develop more sensible, integrated and proactive urban/human strategies. But the times are changed, because we live in the age of a deep metamorphosis: of paradigms (knowledge-based), of horizons (ecological-oriented) and of lifestyles (cooperation-led). After the Industrial Revolution we have entered the Anthropocene, the era of massive human impacts on the planet, able to destabilize Earth's natural systems, with severe consequences on the human settlements. But, in their recent book

Johan Rockström and Mattias Klum (2015) affirm that Anthropocene doesn't mean only an unsustainable human footprint on the earth, but they argue that we have unprecedented opportunities to navigate a "good Anthropocene", by embracing a deep mind-shift, rediscovering common values, and taking on the essential role of planetary steward. In face of anti-urban tensions we must shift towards a **Neo-Anthropocene**, where "anthropos" is the highest expression of human being, where a renewed ethics of political responsibility and a more sensible urbanism focus on being more creative in using natural and cultural resources, smarter in economy, open in governance, intelligent in transport and resilient in living: self-sufficiency, circularity, sharing and recycling are the main keys. In contemporary society, cities could be considered vibrant organisms of space and community, of data and information, of sensors and actuators, of actions and reactions, of urban/rural metabolism generated by people and environment both. Five thousand years ago the city was the best invention of the mankind, thought to be an "enabling device" for community's evolution and innovation, not only a safe place or a symbolic one. During the millenary urban evolution the enhancing role of the city was constantly supported by technology, mechanical first, hydraulic and steam later, electric more recently, and digital in the present age. The smart city revolution, starting as a disruptive and heretic innovation, it became an untouchable tabu (Townsend, 2013), a buzzword in urban planning. Starting from first experiment promoted by technology enterprises, the smart city proposes that technology can be harnessed by municipal administrators to achieve unprecedented levels of monitoring, efficiency, security, convenience and sustainability. But it isn't enough insert the information technology in a traditional urban body to improve the intelligence of cities, and a closer look at several smart cities' practices suggests that such a city will not serve and enhance the interests of the people who live in it.

We need to lay a new groundwork for the far more fruitful alternatives to come, because the role of city as human enhancement must be renewed and reinforced.

In order to not lose the powerful vision of contemporary cities as place enhancing collective intelligent of people we need a paradigm shift able to produce an intellectual toolkit for those of us who want to take the challenge in rethinking the sterile and unappealing vision.
In the post-city age and beyond the smart city, against the anti-urban movement and inside the creative city I want to propose the **Augmented City**: a spatial/cultural/social/economic platform for enhancing our contemporary life, individual and collective, informal and institutional, expanding the urban space generated by the effects of innovation. If we live and act in a reality permanently improved by hard and soft devices, our cities must be more responsive to our behavioral changes. We would be able to build a more efficient urban environment, able to sense, to understand and to act everyday and for everyone.

The Augmented City is an emerging paradigm that perceives the demands of a society more networked and knowledge-based, that answers to the global change and new circular metabolism. Augmented City redefines dogmas of urbanism that we often thought of being more static and rule-based, recovering its prospective, incremental, responsive and creative approach. Augmented City acts simultaneously on cultural, social, environmental and economic components to activate a human/urban regeneration.

The Augmented City is a key enabling space for augmenting people life, it's an enabling platform for human creativity, innovation and equality and for territorial sustainability, economy and quality. In the Augmented City everyday data-capturing devices can monitor rainfall, pollution, water, energy, natural light or traffic, social needs and people life and then process this information in real time, thus allowing for creating a seamless coordination and planning system, and enabling the shared use and optimization of resources. But it's not just about central issue: giving open and collective access to this information will allow people to be more creative, more in sync with the environment and to make decision accordingly. The current challenge in urban planning and design is only defining the places of encounter between the natural and the artificial: the best balance between urban and rural, agriculture and housing, production and consumption. In the next circular challenge, one way of breaking out the linear thought is to create an efficient interface between physical and cyber state. This will allow for the production/management of resources to happen in the same place where raw material is, where production could be local, where energy consumption is near to the renewal resources production, where community behaviour could be informed and empowered.

From monitoring devices to aware information, from information to synchronization with environment and nature, from respect for nature to urban metabolism: this is the "stairway to heaven" from smart devices to living cities, from smart places to enabling city.

In recent decades, bad urbanism was as an inexorable and insensitive Dalek (the famous Doctor Who's enemy) shouting continuously his mantra: "regulate, regulate, regulate", instead of sharing visions, realizing sustainable project and producing stable quality. His weapons were public finance, land consumption, ground and real estate rent and an unbreakable faith in technical rationality, instead of public-private partnership, recycling of resources and empathic approach to community needs. We need to rescue the original meaning of urbanism as quality and welfare producer, its projective dimension and its collective values to improve sense of civic duty and belonging to places.

THE CITY IS THE BEST PLACE WHERE THE IDEAS HAVE SEX

The city has been the best place to live because allowing a community life that build fruitful relationships, generate fertile synapses, producing new economies and accelerating innovation. In his history of innovation, Steven Johnson (2010) draws on seven centuries of scientific and technological progress to show what sorts of environments nurture innovation and creativity. He finds that great creative milieux (whether Los Alamos labs during the Second World War, Warhol's Factory in New York during the Sixties and MIT in Boston today, or Rome in Classical Age, Florence in Renaissance and New York City or Tokyo today, or the web and the social networks) are like coral reefs, teeming of diverse colonies of creators who interact with and influence one another. Cooperation in nature is just as important as competition. That is the secret of the coral reef: everything is recycled in a limited space on a matrix of calcium carbonate built up by the coral – the ultimate example of "bootstrapping": a self-sustaining process able to proceed without external input.

The key to both natural and technological evolution is bricolage: recycling spare parts, taking objects from one context and placing it in another. The most creative environments are those that create a platform for innovation, allowing the greatest number of spare part add-ons, resources to recycle, raw material to remake.

This is what – argues Johnson – unites the coral reef, the Italian cities of the Renaissance (the paradigmatic creative cities) and internet: all are fertile environments that have enabled a myriad innovations. And the city is the best place where these innovations could find necessary tangible/intangible resources, as long as it is able to recover his propensity for creativity and collective intelligence. Cities as powerful creative habitats "are platforms to open doors to the adjacent possible" (Johnson, 2010) and each new urban innovation opening up new ideas to explore.
So what is it that leads to innovation nature, technology or cities? It's the sharing of ideas and building upon them.
Matt Ridley (2010) describes it as "ideas having sex", arguing that socio-economic growth comes from the collision of information and new ideas, shared openly. "The secret of the modern world is its gigantic interconnectedness. Ideas are having sex with other ideas from all over the planet with ever-increasing promiscuity. The telephone had sex with the computer and spawned the Internet", says Ridley. If innovation happens when people keep building on what's been done before, then I like to affirm that *the Augmented City is the best place where ideas have sex*: it has to be planned and created to facilitate the fertile collision of ideas and people, of identity and innovation.
In 2013 TED conference argued that, at its best, contemporary "city 2.0" is hub of human connection, fountain of creativity and exemplar of green

living. Yet at the same time, it still suffers the symptoms of late industrial urbanization: pollution, crowding, crime, social fragmentation and dehumanization. Cities were born and have resisted all alternative proposals – and the storms of post-urban – becoming the prevalent form of human settlement due to their ability to continually create a platform for innovation, allowing the greatest number of spare part, offering recyclable materials with which to build new relationships, or semi-finished places on which to complete the process of metamorphosis.

Metamorphosis is the new powerful keyword of the future cities, and we must accept the challenge to perform it during this transition years. Metamorphosis asks cities are subjected to a perturbation of their tangible and intangible components, acting local and connecting reticular. This disruptive action on cities could reshape their spaces, would reactivate their metabolism, switch on again their generative power and reboot their innovative propulsion.

THE AUGMENTED CITY CIRCLE

To improve the weapons of the good urbanism, we must identify the main components able to reset the urbanism and spatial planning for reimagining the Augmented City in face of the millennium challenges: true antidotes against the Dalek-like urbanism. In front of the deep changes that involve the cities in the Neo-Anthropocene and the new questions that emerge from the urban communities increasingly responsible and active need new answers in a position to act in the metamorphosis we are going through. And the **Augmented City** is the paradigm needed to meet the diverse and multi-scale questions that come from the four main challenges of the cities in the XXI century: the impact of the knowledge society and the expansion of network communities, the answer to climate change and the circularity of the urban metabolism. To understand how Augmented City is a new paradigm capable of responding to the new demands, opportunities and needs of the metamorphosis we are going through, I developed a conceptual diagram, the Augmented City Circle, who orders the components and the respective dimensions on which acts inside of the main issues that the urban planning and design have to face in the changing times. The Augmented City Circle collects and defines the ten main component (focused in following pages), **ten challenges to overcome for augmenting the innovative and creative power of the city as enabling platform, generative environment and knowledge server for communities.**

The Augmented City is a vision/process/project able to respond to four major challenges of the 21st century (the four axes of the Cartesian diagram): the responsive city as a place that can meet the needs of the community in an effective and timely way, the sustainable development as a horizon for the quality of human settlements, the smart land as responsible use of innovation and information technology and the new spatial patterns essential to reshape not erosive forms of human settlements. The axes delimit, then, the four quadrants which define as many goals of human development: the affirmation of the *Knowledge Society* and the expansion of the *Network Society,* the risks of *Global Change* and self-sustainability of the *Urban Metabolism*. Within this logical schema acts the Augmented City Circle through its ten characteristics, each of which produces a specific response in one of the main dimensions of development (knowledge, sharing, innovation, economic, cultural, circular, environmental, connective, metropolitan and incremental). Each of the Augmented City features is placed in quadrants and plays a predominant role in the response to the challenges placed along the axes. For each feature, finally, it is called the prevailing dimension within which it acts, and are synthesized three main spatial, economical, social or cultural devices/tools able to identify concrete actions on the realm of cities and territories. The details and the emerging practices of the ten characteristics of Augmented City will be detailed in the respective chapters of this book.

First an Augmented City is **Sentient** because it uses a wide range of sources for acting by a knowledge dimension to answer several people's questions and to solve several problems. So it needs new values, skills and tools for renewing a knowledge-based and solving-oriented urbanism in a well-timed collaborative scenario. And it's thus also based on **Opensource** approach, because needs for a civic-tech-urban structural alliance in the Sharing Society we live, able to generate new public collaborative space. The city is no more a "pre-compiled code" of spaces and functions, but it is a collaborative and incremental process of meeting places and housing, social infrastructure and places of co-work. And then it triggers a renewed community covenant that reactivates the constituent factors of urban life. In the innovation dimension the Augmented City is **Intelligent** — more ingenious than smart — because it can generate an enabling ecosystem based on the hardware of better urban spaces, on the software of the active citizenship, but overall on an "urban operative system" for an advanced and responsive city planning and design. The fourth keyword is **Productive** because next cities need to reactivate their economic dimension framing the powerful makers movement within a new the creative/productive urban ecosystem for improving the manufacturing renaissance in the cities based on the new "artisan economy" (Anderson, 2012), for reconstituting an essential economic base of the city, after years of euphoria for city as service-provider only. But the city will also be more and more **Creative** improving the cultural dimension through the integrated use of culture, communication and cooperation (3C of the next generation of creative city) as resources for an active city that can generate new forms and pattern able to stimulate the human creativity and able to stimulate a different growth based on identity, quality and reputation. An Augmented City is **Recyclical** because is based on recycling processes and led by circular principles. It asks for a paradigm shift for transition cities that not only re-duce, re-use, re-cycle their tangible and intangible resources, but design a new circular metabolism, by including "planned recycling" among the components of the urban project. In the ecological dimension it is **Resilient**, that means accepting the task for adaptive, circular and self-sufficient cities for winning the climate change challenge, producing and distributing effectively the "resilience dividend" (Rodin, 2014) as effective instrument of urban ecological equalization. The Augmented City is **Fluid** because asks to rethink porosity and fluidity as projective paradigms in the connective dimension for urban regeneration projects that derive by water their charge of identity, producing new spatial configurations from renewing interface port-city not as place-threshold but as a producer of powerful urban identity. In the metropolitan dimension, the **Reticularity** defines the process from a traditional ecosystem and gravitational model to a new and more effective reticular one, based on metropolitan super-organism and rur-urban archipelagos. Last but not least, an Augmented City needs a new implementation approach, an adequate process for allowing to transform ideas into action, for focusing several actions into a holistic vision. It needs a new alliance between public-private-civil society and ask for innovative paths to implementation. So Augmented City must be **Strategic**, asking for an incremental dimension, an adaptive approach and a time-oriented action, able to activate several cycle to regenerate districts, cities and lands. To meet these new challenges I have developed a innovative protocol for urban regeneration, which I call **Cityforming$^©$**, based on a system of incremental colonizing tactics, opensource consolidating actions and development strategies, preferring an approach by an relational-incremental masterprogram rather than a rational-comprehensive masterplan.

These keywords I have defined as many conceptual diagrams that summarize and make it immediately understandable the concepts they represent. The ten components of the Augmented City will define a rich cloud of meanings, tools and good practices of cities that improve their material and immaterial resources and strength their collaborative spaces linking them with the networked communities. Cities that sense and act by its wide and deep networks of human sensors and civic actuators, of technologic devices and smart citizens, of creative actors and productive players.

An Augmented City must be a disruptive – and reconstructive – innovation in urban design, spatial planning and land management, and in everyday life also. We could sketch seven step for improving an **urban agenda for augmented cities and communities** made of policies and their spatial consequences:

1) realize a creative ecosystem connecting talents, education and training starting from interfacing schools, universities, cultural centers and enterprises, so that they become creative hubs and incubators of ideas, projects and innovative jobs, strengthening the institutions/community cooperation between augmented people;

2) make administration and services easily accessible to anyone at any time and from any place by accessing at their spaces and data both to increase the openness, the knowledge sharing and the cooperation to decision;

3) increase and diffuse sensors and actuators for problem monitoring and solving, capable of understanding in real time needs, demands and criticities and allow for a proper and timely solutions in a sentient and active city;

4) plan public spaces and services for different uses and for different users over the day to minimize the costs of management, to maximize efficiency and to ensure the maintenance for a hyper-sharing city that lives of several human / urban metabolisms;

5) channel the energy of active citizenship to the collaborative management of new urban facilities; theaters, museums, libraries, public spaces and welfare services need a public-private-civil society common management for empowering and spreading the civic dimension of the augmented city;

6) facilitate public-private partnerships for the implementation of measures of energy efficiency, sustainable mobility, building security and environmental quality enhancing the fundamental entrepreneurial dimension for enforcing the urban circular economy;

7) facilitate the growth at the neighborhood level of micro-production, digital fabrication, repair and recycling as new job opportunities making city manufacture-based and production-oriented again, after the false myth of the city based exclusively on services.

These seven points of an urban agenda for augmented cities and communities make up the perimeter for politic and planning actions, for business and social activities, for economic and cultural life, able to reshape the city through a renewed paradigm for urbanism.

Augmented City is not just a new definition, but it needs the paradigm shift, that I propose. It needs collect several existing empirical evidence, traces of practices or real experiments.
But above all it needs the continued testing of spatial, social, cultural and economic consequences of urban planning and design enabling the collective intelligence of its inhabitants.

In the following pages are presented some ongoing experiments where I have detected traces of innovation, sparkles of creativity, seeds of change. This book analyses, critics and interprets several places worldwide where institutions, urbanists, activists, communities and enterprises are testing the first forms of the arising Augmented City paradigm. The result is a theoretical and methodological contribute based on a conceptual atlas of territories and cities seen as enabling platform that augment creativity, productivity and well-being of the communities involved, while also augment the resilience and intelligence of places. Augmented City is explored through its ten components in as many chapters that delve into the spatial, cultural, social and economic consequences. Each chapter is introduced by a diagram that summarizes the issues by acting as a conceptual map for understanding the meaning of the urban paradigm shift. The ten component of the Augmented City are declined and depth through scientific reflections and empirical evidences that argue the soundness of the proposed paradigm. Each chapter concludes with a brief review of practices – emblematic cases or epiphenomena – grounding the concepts. The Augmented City arose about seven years ago, but it grows with exponential progression doubling its components, connections and impacts, seeing in last year to one incredible and disruptive acceleration. Each quarter the components of the Augmented City Circle have doubled the previous ones and now we are surrounded

by millions of practices in spread of sensors and intelligent devices, in collaborative design and return of urban manufacturing, in explosion of creativity and increase of resilience, several experiments in recycling of everything, fluidisation and networking of cities and adoption of incremental and adaptive strategies, as described in this book. As the famous Indian Emperor Gupta, we are at the crucial point of having to manage the "second half of the chessboard" in the innovation's progression not to succumb to the explosion of practices. So we need a theory, a new urban paradigm able to understand, connect and manage the role of cities and communities in the augmented Neo-Anthropocene.

What's the post-city? It is the city, augmented!

ACKNOWLEDGEMENT

This book is the result of a long process of reflections, applied researches and planning experimentations started in the last decade during which I tried to understand how the city was changing and what were the forms of the future urban settlements that still could not see at near horizon. A work started around the new generation of creative cities able to generate new creative communities, continued with the need to re-imagine urbanism to plan and design cities and territories more creative, intelligent and resilient, able to respond to the global change. But this book is mostly the result of numerous trips and even more numerous discussions with people like me trying to figure out how the cities are changing and how it should change our profession of urban designers and planners. I am grateful to the cities that have welcomed me and have given me their beauty and their secrets revealed, guiding my search for augmented cities in practice. And I thank the many people who have offered me suggestions, documents and informations, which often comforted me in my intuitions and sometimes changed my mind. Not to mention because they are so many, but I'm sure they will recognize themselves in the book. Finally, this book is dedicated to my daughter Lucrezia, because I want her and her generation to live an augmented city capable of enhancing their creativity, intelligence and sensitivity.

Territorial planning and urbanism are expected to increase their sensibility to read social changes to consequently design new urban settlement forms and, above all, to enhance the ability to identify new demands and new actors resulting from the social metamorphosis: from lifestyle changes to new forms of inequality towards a renewed vision for a sustainable future.

1. SENTIENT

THE SENSE/ACTIVE CITY
Knowledge/solving urbanism for collaborative cities

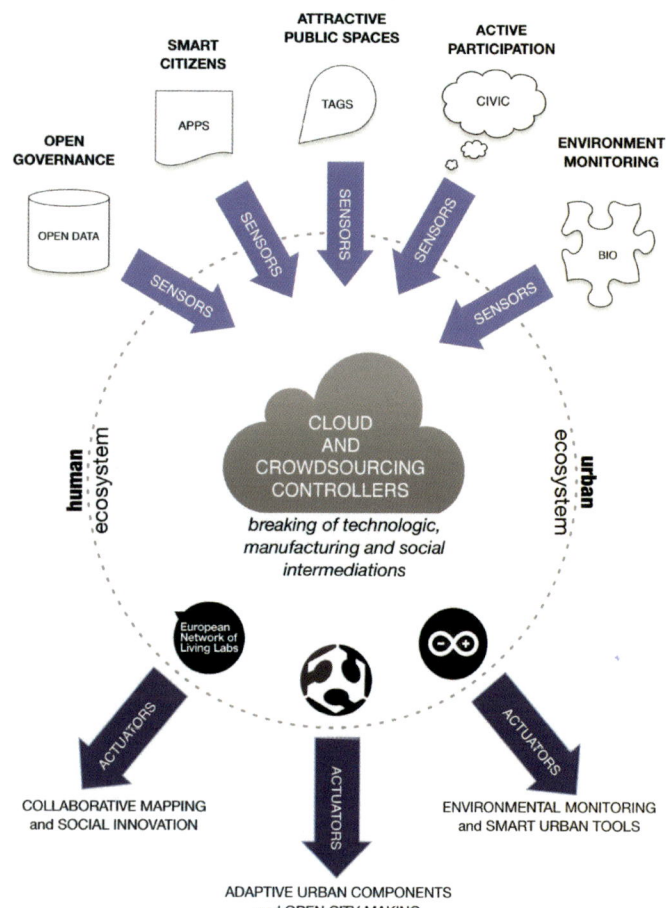

THE PROACTIVE SENTIENT CITY

Regional planning and urbanism are expected to increase their sensibility to read social changes for designing new human settlement forms and, above all, for enhancing the ability to "sense" new demands and actors resulting from the social metamorphosis. The sentient city must interpret lifestyle changes and give answers to new forms of inequality, building a responsive vision for a sustainable future. Which does not merely mean adopting a forward-looking approach, but strengthening the addressing capacities, providing quick and efficient responses to proactive demands. For this to be implemented without resorting to old-style social engineering, local governments are expected to strengthen their ability to be sensible interpreters of needs and guides to development. At the same time, the increasingly wide network of active citizens must be in a position of sharing the responsibility to connect new demands with the associated system of decisions and solutions. Even the new information and communication technologies (which will be further explored) are increasingly contributing to provide monitoring tools for analysis, supporting forecasts and decisions as well as devices stimulating the access to knowledge on the part of the local community, which is increasingly demanding the information gap between policy makers and social actors to be bridged.

A sentient planning process, dialogue-based and cooperative, coupled with cloud governance and collaborative urbanism is the fundamental prerequisite to reverse the supply-demand relationship in the urban project: provision of services, design of spaces, location of functions and performances must be the direct consequence of real demands. As a matter of fact, as long as the offer – that is a bulimic market – influences the market needs, urban policies will continue to lead the city to self-destruction.

The needs expressed by the community become more articulated, intangible and plural, thus requiring a similarly complex and articulated response from local governments, whose analysis is less random and conformist providing more creative and innovative solutions that pave the way to a new era. In a society characterised by turbulent urbanization that is rediscovering the rural dimension, the city will have to find adequate answers to new demands generated by the crisis.

Manuel Gausa wrote on **City Sense** (IAAC, 2012) that "our societies are the most complex dynamic and informational systems that exist: they are space-time (as well as sensorial) systems constantly exchanging information among the elements that comprise them, and between the latter and the environment, mutating and fluctuating in an evolutionary manner". The consequence of this new dynamic and informational urban condition is the city no longer built based on substantive formal criteria about land use, but it is defined and redefined dynamically, continuously, relationally, by an interactive combining of different layers of information (topographic, biological, economic, cultural, environmental, socio-political, etc.).

The proactive and sentient Augmented City is no longer just forms, uses or flows, but rather a complex system of relationships and events in process, among which simultaneous processes of action and reaction, of sensors and actuators are triggered. "The sense-city – argues Gausa – refers to the ability to process projectually the universe of information and transform it, territorialize it and project it into/towards more imaginative and qualitative dynamic spheres of life and relation."

We need not only a new kind of urban planning, but a disruptive urbanism which is more empathetic, sensible and integrated with the environment (more sustainable), with the context (more sensitive), with the people (more involved), with the new creative society of information, exchange and innovation.

The technology has always been based on a technical device that acts as a sensor that through a intermediation of a dedicated master controller allows a tool to implement the resulting action. A one-way relationship and above all enclosed within a univocal relation between the sensor and its actuator: a closed relationship in a gathered world. This was also the traditional "command and control" model, the formal top-down management method for managing our complex urban systems.

But this model has a big drawback: in the open society the individual contributors always have more information and better skills than the leaders, so they are really in the best position to make decisions and to be effective actuators. So we must change from a master controller model to an enabling model based on co-creation. The **Diagram n. 1** shows how it have to be transformed the traditional relationship between sensors and actuators in urban planning and management.

Today the technology of sensors/actuators is changed, opening up to a reticular and distributed approach which has radically changed the appearance. And when the system sensor/actuator acts on the city and on our lives, it needs a radical metamorphosis from a tool mainly technological to a complex system of human/urban sensors and makers.

First of all, we changed the sensors, which are no longer just technological, but are *biological* (derived from environmental monitoring by living being), *civic* (derived from the active citizens' participation) or derived from the *tags* in the most attractive places (often produced by the huge amount of data generated and shared by Ingress and PokemonGO players). Informations are also produced by *apps* used by smart citizens (think the explosion of apps dedicated to urban mobility, more and more community-based as Waze) or come from *open data* produced by institutions and enterprises. This galaxy of sensors is no longer handled by a single controller, but the spread and development of cloud and crowd-sourcing controllers breaks any technology, manufacturing or social intermediation drawing directly to the wide ecosystem of urban and human intelligences (Shepard, 2011). Even the actuators have changed and are no longer just technological tools, but arise from our daily lives, and from the tools produced by the digital revolution. We can identify three families of actuators in the Augmented City. The first includes all those that are powered by **Arduino** processor and allow a permanent environmental monitoring integrating a low-cost CPU everywhere and producing smart tools – even wearable – at low cost and with a high level of adaptability. The second family of actuators consists of **Fab Lab** ecosystem that allow to produce building, mobility or service components that adapt themselves to different situations rather than using an abstract standardization: customisation and tailoring are the new keywords in design processes. The Fab Lab are also the developers of an opensource urban culture to find shared solutions to common problems. To this family of actuators belong the several repair activities that today contribute to the implementation of the circular economy. The third family consists of the **Living Labs** acting in cities such as active components of the bottom-up solution of the problems, spreading education, producing collaborative maps and contributing to the strengthening of social innovation neighborhoods or to reactivate regeneration areas by education activities.

Therefore, using an obsolete command and control model to manage the complexity of a city is doomed to failure. We need to liberate our active citizens, civic leaders and urban professionals to co-create social environment and to plan the city by enabling protocols. We need enabling behaviors based on shared data and crowdsourced knowledge.

PLANNING IN THE DATAFIED SOCIETY

As our world gets increasingly connected and mediatised, input and expertise from the urban and social sciences becomes essential to understanding the dynamics, ethics and pragmatics of the "datafied society", according to the effective Schäfer's definition. Because Open and Big Data are taking place at the core of our culture, economy and social organization, it is crucial that urban planners tackle questions about how this process affects our knowledge, interpretation and design of forms and relations of human settlements, their developments. That datafication is a phenomenon that urgently demands investigation it was acknowledged in urbanism more than a decade ago. The Augmented Cities in the datafied society ask that urban planners have to be able to deploy new skills and methods that come along with this paradigm shift. Significantly, planning professionals need to be educated to become critical data practitioners who are both capable of working with data and of critically questioning the illusions that frame the datafied society. It also means they have to leave the ivory tower and enter the wild world of data practices to witness how they transform institutions, shape business models, and lead to new forms of governance or civic participation. Increasing the data infrastructures is not sufficient, as cities ought to endeavour to increase the rate of collective intelligence, by supporting, via cloud communiting, virtuous behaviour from the bottom and raising the profile of a new way to understand urbanism displaying its individual and collecting benefits.

Smart communities are increasingly characterise by platforms for service whose value lies in the offered facilities considered useful by the users, which in turn translate them into additional services to other users. A sort of mutual complicity is therefore important between the platform and the value-adding users, which can be implemented provided the platform/user relationship is transparent, open and authentic hence included in the new citizenship pact.

The Open Data are indispensable to open governance if they are open to citizens both in terms of transparency and especially of direct participation in decision-making processes, promoting the use of ICT inasmuch as they accelerate the empowerment of communities, virtual in the first place and increasingly real today, other than generating renewed physical spaces fuelled by knowledge, sharing and inclusiveness. According to Manuel Castells (2012) online and offline networks ought to be joined to obtain the new politics for the city as commons. Open and Big Data, the immense amount of data not only from government websites, but from social networks too, from blogs and specialistic websites, if adequately managed and interconnected, allow generating knowledge that could not be possibly obtained through traditional sources. Imagine planning the transport system of a city not only based on the service provider's information, but with the possibility to rely on

users' feedbacks: their tweets, their complaints, thematic blogs, traffic information from the local police, data regarding ongoing or planned construction sites, information about planned strikes and demonstrations, the calendar of major events, citizens location trends and the list could be longer. All of these potential information must be handled within a city model allowing its use in terms of urban planning and design, otherwise they will just be "noise floor".
Data management is not limited to the administrative sphere or to decision-making processes, but requires the traditional urban planning's cognitive model to be revised. It requires us not only to modify the protocols on which we base the plan's knowledge, but also to create new planning instruments. Hence, the first forms of Open-source Urbanism (Sassen, 2011). We should therefore begin to outline it and experience its practices in order to identify the main application protocols. We find ourselves in a smarter dynamic and innovative context therefore. Above all, it is shared and open, and ought to be also more "senseable" – according to Carlo Ratti –, aware and responsible.

A proper cloud governance, not to be turned into a new mantra however: it ought to cooperate with leaderships and technocracies, with the directors and planners of the change, the actors in the transformation and the civil society to understand the extent to which the issue of openness and transparency involve their organizations, be it businesses, institutions, communities or universities.

Areti Markopoulou wrote about the post-machine sense (IAAC, 2012): "the great challenge for a new urban metabolism lies in the capacity of the city to interact, to give and receive information among interconnected nodes of different scales and natures (infrastructure, buildings, public spaces elements, environmental conditions, flows). This anticipates fundamental concepts related to the importance of proposing symbiotic systems of organization based on real time data that can be further articulated into responsive systems and metabolic organizations".

Cities, then, become a knowledge-based organism, consisting of a central brain fed by the sensors' nervous system. Cities become some permanent urban data sourcing: sensors that are able to collect and measure data and that process them to transform into information and to define actions based on efficiency. Several cities are experimenting sensor-based urban planning: districts able to filter water, to manage ventilation and air quality, to locate and balance traffic levels, to process waste in order to produce biofuel and energy.

On the other hand, cities become increasingly citizen-based, capable of incorporating contingencies based on real time information generated by the users. Flexible and temporary public spaces formed according to citizen's needs, urban interfaces for participation planning generated both for and by the users, open data platform for citizens to be more in sync with the environment.

The sentient/active city evolves based on self-organization rules related to crowdsourced local parameters, social, technological or emotional factors of the citizens when occupying space, when doing their activities or when commuting.

Several experiences of urban regeneration in decaying areas indicate that the planning process is increasingly committed to promoting of urban policies aimed at social cohesion, through an appropriate equipment of services, public facilities and improved accessibility, at encouraging the implementation of housing policies guaranteeing the right to housing for the poorest sectors of society, and at strengthening the multi-functional nature, as well as pursuing formal qualities that could thus become positive factors of urban identification. Even the development policies of the inland areas must change approach, urging planning to increase accessibility of natural and cultural resources, to promote urban policies that ensure the right to a creative endeavour to development, promoting networking policies between new patterns of human settlement and pursuing quality landscape design, which is able to trigger virtuous processes of identification and belonging to places, thus strengthening the genius loci's recognition.

To ensure this process of identification and self-representation in the territory, a major emphasis shall be placed on the link between knowledge and action, suggesting a pragmatic "action-oriented knowledge", instead of the traditional "survey-analysis-decision-action" set, thus contributing to put the new urban actors at the core of planning practices, revising the scope of experts' contributions, preferring a network of shared knowledge, expertise and common knowledge when it comes to identifying and solving problems. There is a growing need for a new planning epistemology for interactive and increasingly plural spatial planning/urbanism, capable of managing needs and changes, no longer mandatory in their motivations and obvious in their outcome, hence often incorrect in the motivations and unsuccessful in the outcome, but resulting from a process of dialogue-based and contextual knowledge, empowerment of individuals, shared agreement on the future and strengthening of local actors.

From the point of view of the changes that technical planning skills are undergoing owing to the shared co-planning principle's application, education and research commitments, coupled with professional experiences, will determine the need to explore opportunities – and risks – offered by the tools that are currently presented as solutions to direct participation. Forums and user groups, communicative and participative planning labs, living labs will undergo several and diversified experimentations, not so much aimed at assessing their effectiveness in individual practices, but rather the general effectiveness of protocols and good practices in triggering virtuous emulation and structural changes of administrative processes and projects towards a more sentient and responsive city.

PLANNING BY LIVING DATA

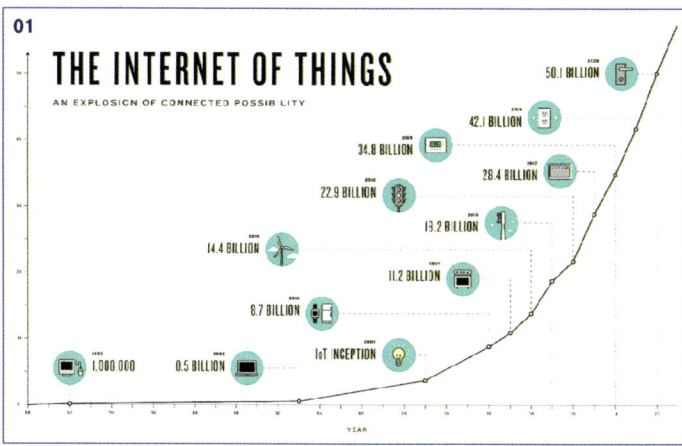

01. 01. The infographic of the explosion of the **Internet of Things** shows the birth of a society based on 50 billions of connected devices: true artificial collective intelligence connecting not only things but the people behind the devices. The city of the future will be infrastructured by several intelligent devices connected to each other and acting as sensors able to interpret and share information about spaces, mobility and people. We are surrounded by Bruce Sterling's Spimes: a location-aware, environment-aware, self-logging, self-documenting, uniquely identified objects that flings off data about itself and its environment in great amount. So, the Augmented Urbanism must act on a universe of Spimes: this huge amount of interconnected informations will allow to plan and manage cities by living data in an effective responsive approach, able to reshape our relations with data and informations in a true internet of cities and communities.

02. Smart Citizen is a platform to generate participatory processes of the people in the cities. The Smart Citizen project is based on geolocation, Internet and free hardware and software for data collection and sharing, and the production of objects; it connects people with their environment and their city to create more effective and optimized relationships between resources, technology, communities, services and events in the urban environment. The project is born within Fab Lab Barcelona at the IAAC.

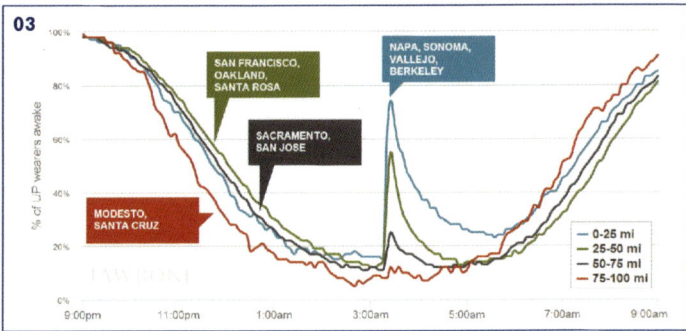

03. Open Data analysis by wearable sensors. The South Napa earthquake was the strongest to hit Northern California in 25 years. The Jawbone data science team wanted to quantify its effect on sleep by looking at the data recorded by **UP bracelet** wearers in the Bay Area who track their sleep patterns. Napa, Sonoma, Vallejo, and Fairfield were less than 15 miles from the epicenter. Almost all (93%) of the UP wearers in these cities suddenly woke up at 3:20AM when the quake struck. Farther from the epicenter, the impact was weaker and more people slept through the shaking. In San Francisco and Oakland, slightly more than half (55%) woke up. Once awaken, it took the residents a long time to go back to sleep, especially in the areas that felt the shaking the strongest.

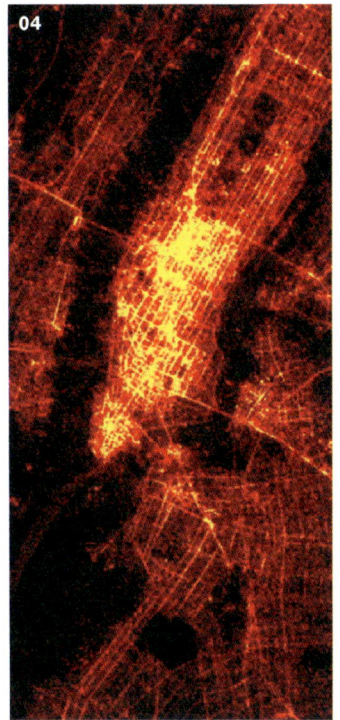 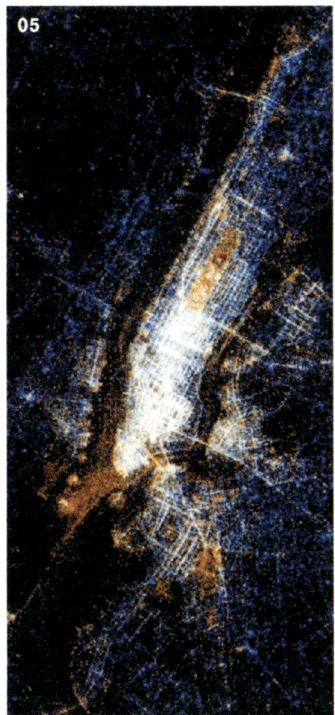

04-05. Eric Fischer's **social maps** show world in a new light: by geotag and open-source tool experts make our hashtags and tweet a little more interesting. Fischer's projects illustrate different global trends: social media usage, taxi trips, and tourist locations around the world, among others. The visualizations of NYC that pulse depicting where people are tweeting the most their everyday life. The New York "See something or say something" map shows the different sensibility of people in reacting to the places: red dots are locations of Flickr pictures, blue dots are locations of Twitter tweets and white dots are locations that have been posted to both. The difference of colours shows the most-photographed places or the most-commented places in the city as a sensor of their relevance. Fischer's vivid maps of race,

traffic, tourism, and crime across the world have drawn international acclaim, each saying something different about ethnicity, commerce, and travel. His work reveals patterns in data that most observers miss.

06. London Map by runners: there are many exercise apps that allow you to keep track of your running, riding, and other activities. Record speed, time, elevation, and location from your phone, and millions of people do this. What about all together? Not only is it fun to see, but it can be useful to the data collectors to plan future workouts or even city planners who make sure citizens have proper bike lanes and running paths. The map allows to know several information about the state of streets, their safety, their attractiveness and the perception of people.

07. Hortus Paris is an interactive environment installed at the EDF Foundation in Paris as part of the Alive exhibition. Its morphology emerges from the reinvention of one of the archetypes of architecture, the column. Imagined as a living and responsive organism, a photo-bioreactor of microalgae, it connects floor to ceiling as part of a continuum landscape of growth and interaction, from photosynthesis to harvest.

08. Showed for the first time in 2012 at the Maker Faire Rome, **St. Horto**, by Francesco Lipari and OFL Architecture, is the first prototype of an interactive garden that creates an ideal synergy between architecture, nature, music and social technologies, producing a living interaction between people and natural environment through several bio-sensors. The innovative feature of

St. Horto is definitely its integration with the 2.0 technology through a customized project. It installs a technology allowing realtime monitoring of the growing plants in the garden, through the use of hardware tools (Arduino with sensors and webcam) and software. In three particular points of the garden, it has been used steel cables which become veritable harp instruments. The evolution is **Wunderbugs**, an interactive architecture based on the human-insect relationship: six spherical ecosystems are equipped with sensors for motion, humidity, temperature and intensity of sunlight and people presence. These data modulate in real time a musical composition implementing an integration between architecture and environment.

09. Progetto **Manifattura – Green Innovation Factory**, by Carlo Ratti and Kengo Kuma, is going to transform a 9 Ha historic tobacco manufacture into a business, innovation and research hub for green building, renewable energy, and environmental technology. The urban approach allows project to give back to the city of Rovereto green space opened to the city: a living/fab lab that ensuring the necessary security for the production buildings, and creating a new large accessible green space. The nearby bike path, which leads to Monaco, ideally connects, as well as physically, this intervention with the most 'advanced industrial conversion centers in Central Europe. New standards in terms of sustainability,

energy efficiency, innovative reuse of spaces and reactivation of productive processes aimed at enhancing the area, are the basis of the new development of the tobacco factory.

10. The **Media-TIC** building, in 22@ Barcelona district, is a meeting point for companies and professionals. Designed by Cloud-9 architect's office, the building seeks to be iconic in the digital world and a vehicle for the dissemination of new technologies, while being designed as a socially open civic space. The ETFE skin is activated using pneumatic mechanisms thanks to luxometer sensors that automatically and independently activate the chamber inflation and deflation devices according to how much solar energy there is. From the beginning of the project in 2000 until 2005, the municipal company 22@Barcelona carried out a project of urban regeneration. After this phase of promoting urban regeneration, a new stage of intense economic and cultural renovation has started: around forty projects are being carried out aimed at creating areas of European excellence in various sectors in which Barcelona can assume international leadership, such as the audio-visual, information technology and communications, biosciences and energy sectors. In this new stage, the 22@Barcelona district is establishing itself as a platform for innovation in business, scientific and cultural activity.

We are increasingly immersed in the society of knowledge, creativity and innovation, today universally regarded as the key to competitiveness, true anti-cyclical factors with respect to the crisis that has overrun the capitalist development protocols which requires processes of knowledge creation, spread and replacement more open and collaborative.

2. OPENSOURCE

THE CROWDSOURCING URBANISM

The civic-tech-urban alliance in the sharing society

A NEW CAMBRIAN EXPLOSION

We are increasingly immersed in the society of knowledge, creativity and innovation, today universally regarded as the keys to competitiveness, true anti-cyclical factors with respect to the crisis that has overrun the capitalist development protocols which requires processes of knowledge creation, spread and replacement more open and collaborative. It requires a constant, powerful and pervasive flow of knowledge, exchange of information, and instant evaluation about the effects of government actions. Innovation has no boundaries, it affects each and every aspect of institutions and enterprises and operates as a "mutagen" of society, requiring a paradigm shift to whom bears the responsibility of governing under the aegis of a renewed leadership. In early 2014 T*he Economist* has published a report about the rise of startups and smart communities, recognizing a new Cambrian Explosion: "digital startups are bubbling up in an astonishing variety of services and products, penetrating every nook and cranny of the economy. They are reshaping entire industries and even changing the very notion of the firm". Fablabs, makers, social innovators, DIY movements and smart citizens have given rise to a global urban movement and most cities now are going to enhance a true collaborative urban ecosystem. The Augmented City is inhabited by hundreds of accelerators and thousands of smart places and co-working spaces, and all these must be highly interconnected in an ecosystem and integrated in a renewed urban metabolism driven by more adequate planning tools (Carta, 2014a). The new path ahead of the world socio-economies today is to draw on the long network flows, transforming them through spatial patterns into energy for local systems. These flows, once diversified into veins of identity, generate value in the local realm to be re-entered in the large global corridors that will thus be revitalised, nurtured, characterized and differentiated. Among the challenges resulting from the connections between global and local, knowledge and skills are the most ambitious and complex. A hope for the future, a generational urgency other than a project for the future driven by knowledge, capacity and inclusiveness, which must work together in harmony.

SHARING KNOWLEDGE AND COLLABORATIVE SOCIETY

The spreading of cities and the improving metropolitan relations need to think of hubs, and how local services can be provided at these hubs, reducing the need to commute or travel in the first place. Commuting distances, congestion tolls, car sharing and pooling, and electric vehicle charging stations are the first examples of how we can evolve to the next stage. Recently, the complex systems that characterize dense cities and reticular urban systems require efficient linkages which reduce friction. So smaller and more specialized transit options are greatly enhanced by today's sharing economy. It reduces the difference and the distance between consumers and producers since, in truth, every one of us embodies both. So consumers are no longer passive, but they'll become active, and whatever they do, they produce value. A collaborative economy harnesses this value and makes the most of it.

Opensource is one of the most powerful trends in urban planning: a new alliance between civicness, urbanism and technology, instead of helping the people who already live better in their neighborhoods, could help themselves and support them in what they need for a better life. "Architectural challenge is to bring the community into the projectual processes" says Alejandro Aravena, Chilean architect and curator of the 2016 Venice Biennale of Architecture. And therefore the Augmented City requires decision-making, planning and management processes more dialogic and collaborative in order to be an enabling platform of development through an alliance among professional, social and spatial components.

The **Diagram n. 2** shows the effects of the addition of urban dimension to the alliance between civic and tech. The diagram has been developed based on a similar one produced by the Knight Foundation (Patel, M., Sotsky, J. et al., 2013) to explore the opportunities of the emerging civic tech landscape. For each economic and social effect selected by the Knight Foundation, we have identified an additional effect on the urban space, a planning process or an urban policy able to produce changes on crowdsourcing city, reshaping the spatial domain.

The first of urban effects concerns the collaborative consumption which is generating the **collaborative city** produced by co-working spaces and co-housing and the dissemination of Living Lab in neighborhoods. The second effect relates to the use of crowdfunding for **public space reactivation**: thousands of citizens contribute financially to the redevelopment of their living spaces and work, build playground for their children, maintain the dignity and safety of neighborhoods by consolidating more and more effects of the sharing economy.
The third alliance relates to the use of social networks to strengthen the birth of a crowdsourcing urbanism feeding of tacit and experiential knowledge of citizens and that transfers to local governments through the **electronic town meetings and forums**, especially in their version of deliberative. The fourth effect acts on the urban community organizing through the explosion of **social streets**, the residential community created to improve the lives of those who live in the same street or in a same block in providing services to the family or to the health and who today are increasingly vital energy of creative districts. The last alliance of civic, tech and urban regards the government data and the improvement of the performance of local authorities response. The results is the extension of the traditional concept of **urban centers** from places of exposure for urban development projects to active sites for open urban policy, for sharing of diagnosis and above all for construction of a real urban governance.

Within a new political vision based on sharing knowledge, skills' impact may take various forms. The pervasive presence of the media, the wireless connection and the increasingly geolocalized social networks changes the way we communicate, think, feel, asses and decide.

Consequently, the expertise possessed by knowledge workers needs strengthening, and the same applies to knowledge leaders. It is not a matter of cognitive and rational practice, but rather of emotion, relationship and ethics other than the ability to understand, guide, change and mobilize diverse knowledge in order to deliver increasingly collective results. In order to provide leaders with the necessary tools to understand the dynamics they are about to implement, the socio-cultural know-how is a fundamental prerequisite. Several practices and experiments demonstrate cognitive and leading force of crowdsourcing not only building common opinions or working together through the network, but producing a true "crowdpolitics": a widespread policy constantly enveloping us both as electors and decision-makers, as askers and responders, thus eliminating distances while reducing the pondering spaces. The 2012 TED Prize winner video about the City 2.0 calls to "combine the reach of the cloud with the power of the crowd" to meet the challenges of the 21st century cities.

Detroit, for example, is trying to rebirth after the social hurricane produced by the death of the automotive industry and the consequent financial collapse through several initiatives of collaborative urban policies. A civic-tech partnership is creating the most comprehensive map of any city in the US, the better to weed out blight: through an interactive website everyone can see every property in Detroit, its condition, and a recent sale price. Thanks to a $1.5 million donation by JP Morgan Chase Foundation, nearly 200 people spent nine weeks crawling every street in the city, and to keep the map up to date they are creating an app that anyone can use to report a blighted building by snapping a photo and texting it in.

DIY CITY AND OPEN SOURCE URBANISM

Political action and politicians' reaction merge in a short circuit that produces a virtuous participation on the one hand, and a vicious fragmentation of decision on the other hand. Not only do changes affect the economic and relational realm, but they are being, with growing pervasiveness, transferred to the physical realm, as regards physiognomy and physiology of intelligent cities. However, a smarter city is not the one whose traditional organization boasts the most intelligent and efficient technology, but the city that profoundly alters the development dynamics

and revisits its housing and mobility patterns rethinking its metabolism through efficient urban cycles.
In times of crisis the sharing economy is achieving important results and dimensions, both in the sharing of goods, services, information, space, time, or expertise, both in the bartering between individuals but also between companies, both in the crowding, but also in the making from hobby to digital fabrication. All that is radically transforming the areas of tourism, transport, energy, and food. But it is the urbanism that through creative and spontaneous forms of DIY – and Do It Together – is reactivating not only places but also flows and activities, and therefore economies. Groups of residents, but also temporary users, travelers, hackers and urban guerrilla gardener reactivate space, manage abandoned places, take care of public spaces, maintain or co-manage collective services through more formalized forms of tactical urbanism that disciplinary culture must not ignore to do with it (Ratti, 2015).
Contemporary cities are the result of numerous demands in terms of housing, work, services, and increasingly care and security, beauty and quality, happiness and innovation, participation and democracy. And the response to these demands is increasingly less institutional and formal: on the contrary, it is rather becoming a collective response characterised by the pro-active involvement of citizens. Urban policies shall take into account not only the different users of the city, such as residents, commuters, city users, metropolitan businessmen, migrants and nomads, but mostly of the new producers of city. Makers, fablabers, urban farmers, startuppers, smart citizens and co-workers are the new protagonists of the contemporary city, acting in the urban, political and social stage of the third industrial revolution, which we have just entered. Citizens become producers, farmers enlivening dismissed and vacant areas through urban agriculture, knowledge workers through workshops or creative incubators, cultural events organizers through crowdfunding, managing theatres and cultural services. They are the new craftsmen of the digital revolution, thanks to their skills in turning with 3D printers, or in fixing objects at a time when recycling becomes more important

than scrapping. These citizens/makers raise awareness of the new landscape, environment and energy saving sensitivity, renewing the traditional role of associations, no longer confined to pointing out the problem, but rather forming part of the solution, bearing its burden in an active and accountable way (Sennet, 2012).

These active citizens are no longer limited to act within their skills or to take care of their places, but they become actors in the new urban scene. The DIY urbanism makes its way to become not only a reaction to the lack of political or technique action but an active component for more effective urban policies and technical actions. An Augmented City has to develop these self-help organizations, commons, social innovation, peer-to-peer, self management, bottom-up initiatives, civic economy, and sharing into a key driver for sustainable development and participatory democracy. Answering to the question: should the authorities provide space for these kind of initiatives or do we then risk the reduction of our public services and our social welfare model?

Today's world cities deal with many problems related to rapidly increasing societal, cultural, technologic and economic transformation processes. More variableness in economic, political and cultural patterns leads to new expectations and renewals of the city in searching for creative solutions by flexible urbanism and architecture: the so called "pop-up city". But we need these initiative to survive the dawn of the next day.

Malaga, in Spain, represents a good practice to stabilize the intervention of the community and make permanent actions for public spaces regeneration. The middle-size city, through the EU Project USER, is empowering community through urban regeneration and is making long-term redevelopment of the slums through the involvement of the population. The testing areas are the old districts Trinidad and El Perchel, places where urban decay and conflict coexist along with rich traditions and social movements active over the past decades. Since 1994 has started a rehabilitation plan which provided for testing a mixed public-private partnership for the old courtyards (the *corralones*) actively involving residents in their management and care. The neighborhood community have begun to take care of their buildings, to keep them clean and decorating them also participating in festivals and competitions to showcase their successes to his fellow citizens and to an increasing number of tourists. In 2004, the project was relaunched through the creation of a People's Museum District to capitalize the renewed local traditions as tourist value and at the same time to promote social rebirth. The experiment has demonstrated the strength of the public space, in a context of social exclusion and conflict, to be a strong factor in urban and social regeneration extending to the streets and squares the sense of identity and belonging that residents already felt for their own backyards. But the value of the project is in management mode through a massive use of crowdsourcing urbanism. For the first time they were put in the field tools such as walking diagnostic, workshops and relations of perception. All assisted by the local support group made up of professionals, representatives of local associations and some popular and peculiar people of the area. The continuous involvement of key actors needs to keep the spaces alive and consistent with their context, but especially to generate a new crowdsourced community of urbanists.

In late 2014 the City of **Paris** launched an open competition for innovative urban project called "Reinventer Paris", offering 23 sites to all professionals where they can develop their ideas and express their talents. The proposals of crowdsourcing urbanism are in terms of housing and everything relating to density, desegregation, energy and resilience, in order to find new collective ways of working that will give shape to the future metropolis. The objective is to seek out, for each site, the most pertinent type of innovation and reveal cutting-edge solutions. "First of all innovation in terms of usage, designing pluralistic buildings that are adaptable and intelligent – declares Jean-Louis Missika, Deputy Mayor of Paris – and the rapid changes in city life styles call for innovation in ways of living, revealing shared and user-friendly spaces, in ways of working, thanks to co-working, teleworking, incubators of a new kind, and in ways of doing business, with shared showrooms, fablabs and ephemeral shops. Invent new services adapted to the health and ageing demands."

Another recent experiment in collective urban design is the **Boston** initiative "New Urban Mechanics" (NUM), a network of civic innovation offices across which explore how new technology, designs and policies can strengthen the partnership between residents and government and significantly improve opportunity and experiences for all. Boston's NUM focuses on four major issue areas with a correspondent laboratory: a) the *Education Lab* explores how new programs and new technology can improve student achievement; b) the *Engagement Lab* explores ways to deepen the connection between city government and its citizens by closer integration and communication between new technology and a resurgent spirit of civic engagement. The ways to improve this connection are by piloting new programs for community deliberation and empowerment, increasing government transparency through both data and story telling and deepening the relationship with universities as a source of new ideas and talents; c) the *Streetscape Lab* is focused on making public space more beautiful, exciting and fun, making parking easier, and improving mobility options and awareness by the integration of green building standards with smart sensor networks. NUM is also experimenting with new designs in public spaces, including everything from new public benches, to new platforms for public art, to new methods to engage artists; d) the *Economic Development Lab* is focused on supporting Boston to be the best place for new and small businesses and to keep housing affordable for all families. In the field of open source urban design acts the project Human Cities led by the Cité du Design in **Saint-Étienne**, aimed to experiment new processes and forms for urban regeneration based primarily on the human capital as empowered actors and not only collector of social needs. The project has stimulate the birth and development of several initiative such as Hypermatière in Saint-Étienne, La Piana in Milan, Demo Graz Ya in Graz and School as a Service in Espoo, that are testing the added value of a bottom-up approach related with a comprehensive vision of the city. Human Cities' approach aims to drive the DIY changes to impact both people and places like shops, public squares, parks, or streets in town and city centres.

The Augmented City is a powerful synaptic structure connecting different thoughts and preferences regarding community building. Being aware that planning should stop relying on authoritarian forms and tools to include participatory processes, which take into account the project's values as expressed by the interconnection among the various actors involved in the plan does not by itself indicate the right way to implement a real and informed participation of citizens in the evolution of physical territory and the community.

In the Augmented City opensourcing is the fourth option among the famous Hirschman's three responses to decline in organisation: exit (emigration and withdraw from the relationship), voice (protest and proposal for change) and loyalty (active participation to governance). It is not only a cost-benefit analysis of whether to use exit or voice led by loyalty to an urban community and heritage identity. Opensourcing is an active contribute to build a collaborative and open code in urban organisation (spatial, social and economic), able to regenerate the city and give a swing against decline. People's rights, needs and desires can not be entrusted to an unique system of representative democracy, but requires a subsidiary approach guided by the principle of educational function performed by the territory, which encourages its inhabitants to knowledge and exploration, self-promoted transformation and renewal through the huge natural and cultural educational potential; and also by the principles of equity and solidarity, longstanding core values of urban planning, able to drive the evolution of city and territory whose quality is made available to all, ensuring authentic forms of participation for active citizens, promoting protection and integration of common interests and reducing associated conflicts.

OPEN SOURCE URBANISM

01. The **New Urban Mechanics** is a network of civic innovation offices. Across the network, we explore how new technology, designs and policies can strengthen the partnership between residents and government and significantly improve opportunity and experiences for all. While the language may sound new, the principles of New Urban Mechanics - collaborating with constituents, focusing on the basics of government, and pushing for bolder ideas - are not. Currently, there are two offices that are part of the New Urban Mechanics network: Boston and Philadelphia.

02. Tactical Urbanism is an umbrella term used to describe a collection of low-cost, temporary changes to the built environment, usually in cities, intended to improve local neighbourhoods and city gathering places. Tactical Urbanism is also commonly referred to as guerrilla urbanism, pop-up urbanism, city repair, or D.I.Y. urbanism. A MOMA's great exhibition "**Uneven Growth: Tactical Urbanisms for Expanding Megacities**" brings together six interdisciplinary teams of researchers and practitioners to examine new architectural possibilities for six global metropolises: Hong Kong, Istanbul, Lagos, Mumbai, New York, and Rio de Janeiro. Uneven Growth seeks to challenge current assumptions about the relationships between formal and informal, bottom-up and top-down urban development, and to address potential changes in the roles architects and urban designers might assume vis-à-vis the increasing inequality of current urban development.

03. Data is everywhere and increasingly a part of our lives. We create it, store it, read it, send it, print it, and erase it on a constant basis- and while much of it may seem trivial or fleeting, there's a surprising amount of data that every individual shares in public digital realms that can be used to better our lives. It's exactly this premise that led the Royal Institute of British Architects (RIBA) and Arup to spearhead an initiative that collects and processes our publicly shared data as a means to design the cities of our future. As permanent citizens of a cyber-grid, we produce, often times inadvertently, specialized maps that describe how we use and interact with our built environment. RIBA and Arup have created a report that made three recommendations to the government in order to reconfigure the current governmental/political systems to work with these new strategies: a) to improve coordination between governmental departments; b) facilitate the digitization of the planning process; c) governing bodies should work hand in hand with the urban planning organizations, that is to say the experts, that focus on the building and planning process with specific insights into the digital world. The image represents the "**London social and functional analysis**", edited by Sir Patrick Abercrombie in 1943 for the Greater London Plan. A simplification of the communities and open space survey showing the existing main elements of London. Around the centre consisting of the port city and west end are grouped the residential communities which are divided into a) the central communities around the west end, b) the east end & south bank communities which have a high proportion of obsolescent property and in the main are adjacent to or mixed with industry, c) the suburban communities the major open spaces and industrial concentrations are also shown.

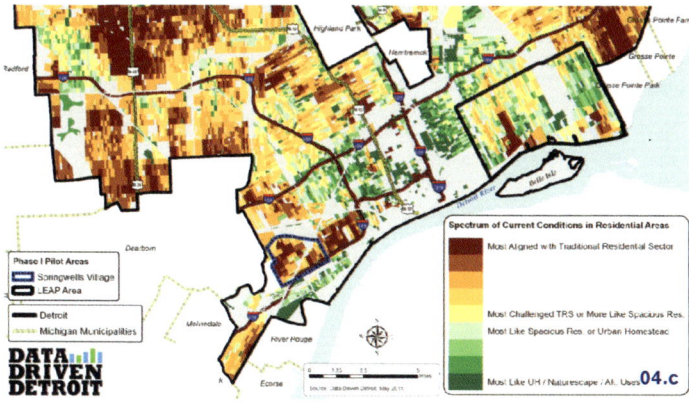

04. Data Driven Detroit (D3) is a statewide organization with a focus on the city of Detroit. D3 houses a comprehensive data system that includes current and historic demographic, socioeconomic, educational, environmental, and other indicators. This data system allows analysts to illustrate complex relationships by combining different datasets to reveal the true stories of our regions, cities and blocks. D3 is committed to serving all communities by adapting data into different formats for different audiences.

05. Human Cities is an European project launched in 2015 by Saint-Étienne, Unesco Creative City of Design. The project, financed in the field of Creative Europe, is a platform of interdisciplinary exchanges of 12 partners led by Cité du Design from Saint-Étienne, that explores the way in which the inhabitants reclaim the constantly evolving contemporary city (especially through experiments in the public space) and ways of re-imagining city life, as sources of wellbeing and quality of life. It's experimenting a revolutionary approach to spatial and services design, not only testing some open source projects for urban regeneration but demonstrating the higher impact of human reactivation in new creative and innovative metabolism of declining parts of cities. One of the most relevant results in Saint-Étienne is **Hypermatière**, a group made up of different structures and people from the Crêt-de-Roch District. Through collaborative artistic projects and solidarity services on Neyron area, it enables inhabitants to be creative actors of the transformation of their district, whether than worried spectator. The Hypermatière project allows to highlight a space in movement on the scale of a neighbourhood, showing the process and the relevance of these contributing practices. Hypermatière offers mobile, evolutive, reversible and recyclable interventions to experiment the various temporalities linked to the uses that accompany the development of a changing neighbourhood. Among the Hypermatière activities one of the most interesting is the mapping of indigenous plant species in the district to educate citizens on the value of urban resilience. The casts of the registered plant species have now become of art installations along the roads. To help urban communities to use the toolkit drawn up by the project to develop open source projects for urban regeneration was opened in 2017 along the central Rue de la République a Human Citizens Office with living lab functions to educate and involve the population.

reinventer.*paris*
Appel à projets urbains innovants

06. Paris has lost its top-down approach to urban regeneration and is going to develop one of the most mature open source processes for reactivate disused areas. So in 2014 the Mayor Anne Hidalgo has launched the **Reinventer Paris Initiative**, a call for innovative urban projects in order to prefigure what the Paris of tomorrow might be. Each team was invited to present its complete projects on how to bring added vitality to exceptional 23 Parisian sites. The vision was that Paris must be able to reinvent itself at every moment in order to meet the many challenges facing it. Particularly in terms of housing and everything relating to density, desegregation, energy and resilience. The initiative aimed to find now collective ways of working that will give shape to the future metropolis. In 2016 75 projects have been selected to compete in Phase 3. Then the winners will be able to purchase or rent the terrains in order to carry out their projects while simultaneously conducting an urban regeneration experiment on large scale. Among the winning projects of the preliminary phase, **Realimenter Massena** by DGT architects proposes a devices based on a circular agro-metabolism from farm to table. The former Masséna Station occupies a strategic position in Left-Bank Paris, one of the major development areas in Paris. Its architecture and location make it a unique pivot point between old and modern Paris. The proposal held the site to play its great potential to become a future focus of activity in the heart of a district that is in the throes of renovation. Another winning project is the **Etoile Voltarie** by Olivier Palatre et Atelier Roberta for the former Parmentier electricity sub-station, built in the early 20th century and emblematic of the Parisian heritage. The proposal takes up the challenge of inventing the cinema of tomorrow, promoting the emergence of a popular and high-quality cinema while simultaneously reflecting on new ways of using or operating cinemas as a community device for enhancing place storytelling. The innovative character

is revealed in the quality of the architectural interpretation by potentially raising the height of the building while preserving and enhancing the current façade.

The Smart City paradigm appears as the best dreamscape, able to put good technology in everyday life, able to transform every people in a smart citizen that senses, checks and acts. We know that an intelligent city is not a mantra or a wishful thinking, but is a projectual challenge to reboot the collective intelligence of the city, the social and the spatial both, and not only the technological.

3. INTELLIGENT

THE INTELLIGENCE OF CITY
Smart planning protocol for multilevel urban tools

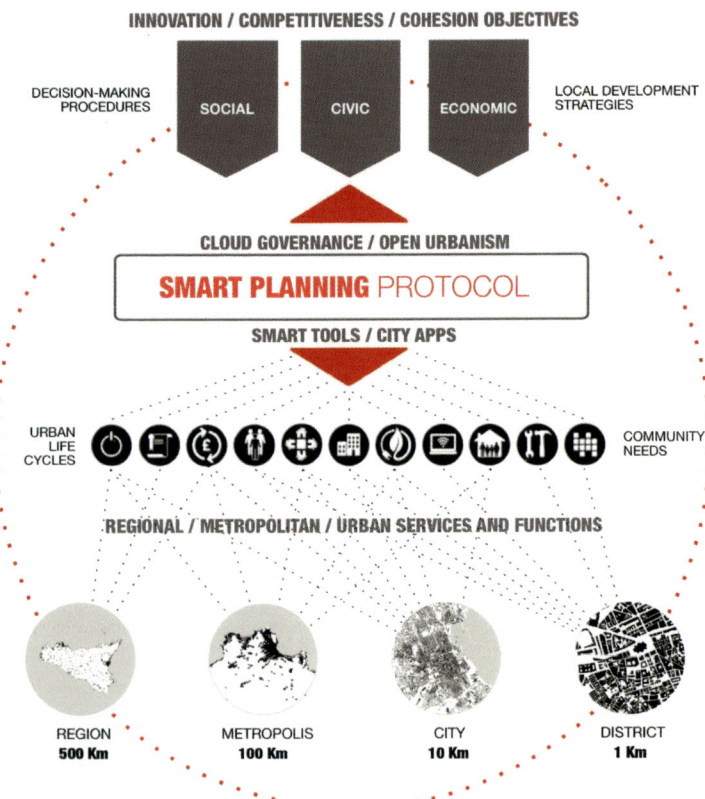

EVERYDAY URBAN TECHNOLOGY

"Urban paradigms are urban dreamscapes, full of wishful thinking about better urban worlds", says Klaus Kunzmann (2014). The Smart City paradigm appears as the best dreamscape, able to put good technology in everyday life, able to transform every people in a smart citizen that senses, checks and acts. We know that an intelligent city is not a mantra or a wishful thinking, but is a projectual challenge to reboot the collective intelligence of the city, the social and the spatial both, and not only the technological. The concept of the Smart City is a "fuzzy concept", with a fluid meaning: there is no absolute definition of an intelligent city, but rather some political, planning, social and economic processes by which cities become more liveable and resilient and, hence, able to respond quicker to new challenges.

We are in the Second Machine Age (Brynjolfsson, McAfee, 2014) where we live, work, move and evolve "surrounded by brilliant technologies". Computers and other digital advances are doing for our ability to use our brains to understand and shape our environments what the steam engine and its descendants did for muscle power: they're allowing us to blow past previous limitations and taking us into new territory. Digitization is improving the physical world, and these improvements are only going to become more important. Second Machine Age involves the automation of a lot of cognitive tasks that make humans and software-driven machines substitutes, rather than complements. Everyday, we witness the application of information and communication technologies to various areas of urban daily life: time management, traffic control, distribution and location of services, bureaucracy streamlining, dissemination of knowledge and communication, monitoring of the environment, not to mention the surrogate social and professional relationships by social networks. Technological innovation applied to production processes, remote home automation, explosion of mobile communications and the Internet of Things, through which by 2020 will be over 50 billion connected devices, will make available with ever-increasing pervasiveness services' delivery and efficient management. In this way,

urban services are first to be enhance for contributing to manage urban complexity, thus ensuring communications, relationships, dissemination of knowledge and empowered citizenship. We have entered the Datafied Age, characterised by a daily increase in the number of databases and maps – often from institutional sources – available in digital format, not only intended for traditional institutional users or experts, but available for multiple uses, open to all potential users and for unpredictable uses. The diffusion of ICT throughout spatial planning processes marks the transition from a merely instrumental role in land management to a quality role in the management of transformations and in the participation, interpretation and orientation of new urban sustainable scenarios.
ICT advantages within planning and management processes are especially clear today, as maps, data and assessment models are increasingly becoming a common heritage: the integration of web and wiki technologies with GIS applications is a very fruitful way to improve the chances of constructive interaction between citizens, policy makers and the wise skills at stake within the urban planning processes. Open data, collaborative mapping and georeferenced systems are central to decision-making processes at local and regional level, facilitating decisions of institutional and entrepreneurial actors, for example by sharing land knowledge, encouraging fast-tracking of administrative procedures. Shared databases can encourage public-private partnerships and project financing by making data, information and feasibility studies available to technical offices or by ensuring multi-utilities contributions.

E-GOVERNANCE FOR ALL

Today, a growing number of communities employ GIS tools to test – with increasingly widespread and interesting results – e-governance practices, which are the innovation of community services not only to provide a greater efficiency, but to increase urban rights, as new interface of the relationship between city and community, a planning method based on extended participation in the emerging forms of active citizenship and, finally, on the balance between cognitive opportunities offered by collaborative urban mapping. The spreading and integration of Web/GIS platforms in the public administrations and the popularity of open data not only contributes to improve the interpretation of resources and their better management, but encourages the establishment of a network of cities aimed at promoting local development, the enhancement of community and businesses services, by strengthening ties with networks of cities at international level. In addition, the cross-platform sharing of land use knowledge increases opportunities for new working activities, meaning opening up new spaces for higher education, lifelong learning and for the repositioning of broad professional categories of workers, especially young.

The development and spreading of new technologies in the field of urban and regional planning shall lead to the experimentation of new interfaces: representation and communication methods enhancing traditional systems to extend the application of geodata within the planning process. In this way, the planning process would change through new modalities to read and understand macro regions, strategic platforms, local systems and on-going socio-economic relations, revealing concealed links which would lead to a non-institutional redefinition of territorial aggregations.

The experimentation, carried out in several local realities, of GIS network projects, aimed at promoting networking of cities, is included within the broader challenge of promoting cloud governance as a new dimension of local development. Community is the sphere of ICT integration into urban policies where the communicative potential is best expressed, and added value is ensured, namely the combination of actors who, out of a common interest, interact within networks by carrying out transactions and exchanges, reporting problems and sharing solutions, developing projects and promoting actions aimed at increasing the added value. Land management as a system of interconnected sensors, together with interfaces and City Apps, for example, can encourage the setting up of virtual districts (in the fields of production, tourism, food, culture) based on cloud computing dedicated to SMEs with the goal of restoring the local system's competitive advantages, stimulating the region's integrated development by linking businesses with other global enterprises networks. The local districts philosophy will lead city networks to compete in the global market as local network systems, employing three important competitive resources: geolocalised information, digital connections and citizen networks.

The combination of technological innovation and urban planning, however, is not only instrumental and determines changes within the community and its territory too. The Third Industrial Revolution and the implementation of the i-society has made it possible to delegate an increasing number of physical and intellectual tasks, even very sophisticated, to technology. In fact, the goods and ideas produced are increasingly less tied to a scheduled place and time, in terms of quality and quantity; the workplace is no longer an independent variable and time is no longer rigidly synchronized, especially as far as the intellectual work is concerned.

URBAN CYBER/PHYSICAL SPACE

The spreading of sensors, electronic networks and urban life apps has created a proper urban cyber-physical space, consisting of the constant interaction between physical components and digital networks, tangible actions and intangible feedback. "We are at the onset of a hybrid dimension between the digital and material world, where the Internet is invading the physical space" – claim Ratti and Sassen (2009) – by identifying it, making it attractive and setting it up for social uses, which are expected to gather the citizens in smart places connected to the network and providing services. We are witnessing the evolution of the cyber cafés: mobile connection disengages the user from a fixed location and brings him back into the city, parks, waterfront and squares allowing him to communicate and interact, learn and point out, know and judge. The dematerialization of technology and its on cloud and mobile spreading allows citizens to "re-materialize" themselves in the city.

The associated research and planning efforts provide a complex framework ranging from the debate on the effects of technological innovation to the analysis of changes occurring within the location of urban settlements and productive activities or in the structure of transport networks and the related infrastructures.

Social and economic transformations, brought about by information and communication technologies, lead planners to investigate changes in resources' exploitation and the evolution of certain qualitative aspects of territorial organization (especially with regard to education and leisure structures).

Finally, opportunities offered by the information society provide planning and land management with new tools, resources, real and virtual subjects. Consider, for example, the growing role of civic networks in the processes of communication and participation in the plan. ICT applied to collective decisions to monitor the effectiveness of the actions, understanding processes and promoting partnerships returns citizens their leading role in the civil society, thus contributing to an adequate distribution of the powers of the plan.
Introducing technologies, protocols and communication digital devices in the urban organism is not only an opportunity for innovation and participatory cognitive processes but should provide an opportunity to redefine development, competitiveness and cohesion in order to give the city a swing power able to overcome the tsunami of the crisis. The *Sidewalk Labs*, founded in **New York** by Dan Doctoroff and Google, is an urban innovation company that will develop technology at the intersection of the physical and digital worlds, with a focus on improving city life for residents, businesses and governments. New technologies, ubiquitous connectivity and sharing, dynamic resource management and flexible buildings and infrastructure are emerging to allow cities and citizens to tackle problems in real time. New technologies are already transforming commerce, media and access to information. Sidewalk

Labs will develop new products, platforms and partnerships to making transportation more efficient and lowering the cost of living, reducing energy usage and helping government operate more efficiently. Beyond the smart city's rhetoric and marketing, the future is challenged to focus on true intelligent cities, as long as they manage to gather skills, generate creativity and innovation incubators empowering communities, in addition to being drivers of competitiveness. Otherwise they risk becoming just "cemeteries of obsolete machines" as fears Saskia Sassen (2011), who is suggesting hacking the city to facilitate its transformation through informal actions performed by the citizens' collective intelligence.

The cyber/physical space is characterized by new actors: the data centers that are flooding worldwide the rural landscape and reusing brownfield sites to handle the immense amount of cloud data required by the intelligence of the cities. No type of building embodies 21st-Century culture more distinctly than the Data Centers – writes Kazys Varnelis (2014) – almost imperceptibly, we've let these telematic spaces into our lives. The physical reality of the cloud, they are the substance behind the portable, networked devices that we peer into as we stumble about our daily business. While data centers house both our public, if nonphysical, gathering spaces and our private refuges, their builders have little interest in treating these structures as works of architecture. The data centers' landscape – a true techscape – is growing fast, infrastructuring the suburbs and often contributing to the reactivation of declining areas. Data centers are becoming architecture of the new smart landscape. They are conceived as environmentally sustainable buildings and often as power generators for the communities.

INTELLIGENT CITY 5.0: COLLABORATIVE, SMART AND CREATIVE

Smart City arose as a vision (the 1.0 generation), then it became a profitable label for technology companies (2.0), and a relevant agenda for national and local governments (3.0), then a planning routine (4.0) for many cities aiming or forced to introduce new intelligent urban infrastructures. But now we need a new generation shift, because a Smart City is not only more intelligent, technologically managed and efficient, but more skilled, fair and equal (Bullard, 2007) which profoundly innovates its sources of knowledge, dialectic capacity, development dynamics and revises its settlement patterns.

The Smart City 5.0 passes from being reactive to proactive by effectively using a better and broader information flow. It invests in people – men and women before human capital – enhancing their ability to empower the social capital, strengthening participation processes, extending education and spreading culture by improving the new mobile communications infrastructures (Campbell, 2012). It focuses simultaneously on software and hardware, to ensure a higher quality of life for all citizens with an accountable resources management through cooperative governance practices. They are defined Smart and Creative Cities (Carta, 2014a) as they will have to be able to innovate high-impact areas: planning, urban design and land management, energy production-distribution-consumption cycle, transport of goods, development of mobility for people and freight, buildings energy efficiency and active participation.

Complex realms, involving several actors such as education, health, waste as well as the enhancement and use of the cultural heritage and tourist attractiveness will have to be innovated. However, cities can not limit themselves to their infrastructures, but shall contribute to increase the rate of "collective intelligence".

Moreover, a city that aspires to be skilled and resourceful needs to show solidarity too, supporting, through cloud communiting, bottom-up virtuous behaviours from below by emphasising the individual and collective benefits of open urbanism.

The challenge of the fifth generation smart cities was accepted by **Barcelona 5.0**: a visioning project based on production, talent and networks as active resources to regenerate the city of the future. According Tomas Diez, one of the initiators of the Fab Lab Barcelona project, the recent changes in Catalan capital have been morphological, geometrical and spatial, based on speculative models called PITO (Product In, Trash Out). The future of Barcelona will be in the optimization of networks, the value of knowledge and energy production and sharing, based on intelligent networks of people and things: the DIDO model (Data In, Data Out). But it's in United Kingdom that big data and technology offer huge potential for cities to deliver services and address some of their principal challenges, such as climate change and environmental sustainability. Over the last few years, several British cities have been proactive in establishing smart city initiatives to reduce emissions and energy consumption. For example, Milton Keynes, through *MK:Smart*, and Bristol, through *Connecting Bristol Scheme*, are both using data collected through several sensors to meet environmental targets in their cities. **Manchester** has launched the *Triangulum project*, a smart city vision for three European cities. Led by Fraunhofer IAO and funded by £4.5 million of European Commission funds, the project aims to create smart districts in Manchester, Eindhoven in Holland, and Stavanger in Norway. This scheme offers a new approach, bringing together a number of green initiatives in one area of the city to test the potential of new technologies. *Triangulum* aims to transform Oxford Road in Manchester (also known as the "Manchester Corridor", the city's student district) as an exemplar for smart technology. There will be a particular focus on reducing carbon emissions, including technologies to improve energy use in buildings and encouraging the use of sustainable transport. An autonomous energy grid for heat and electricity will be introduced alongside a centralised control platform, which will allow Manchester to manage its energy in a localised, energy efficient manner. The system will also allow the city to identify new revenue sources and savings for the system, improving energy and resource efficiency. The project is being led by Manchester City Council, in partnership with the University of Manchester, Manchester Metropolitan University, software provider Clicks and Links, and technology provider Siemens. As a test-bed for green technology, this five-year project will seek to contribute to a small but growing bank of knowledge to help cities find intelligent solutions to deliver more efficient and effective public services. In **Singapore** data is the new currency, and with the spread of open data the city is state of art in smart planning and in data-oriented decision making, transforming itself in a "datacracy" that we observe with interest but also with concern. The wise use of knowledge provided by smart technologies is a challenge to cities and future citizens. Future urban planners have to be aware of what is gradually emerging in their professional filed and planning schools will have to reconsider their curricula, to prepare their students for the new challenges. The discourse on the Smart City promises an era of innovative urban planning, driven by smart urban technologies that will make cities safer, cleaner and, above all, more efficient. Smart Cities will "sense" behaviour via big data and use this feedback to manage urban dynamics and fine-tune services. As in the dream of Patrick Geddes, city planning will become a permanent process, with cities serving as living labs for new products and services. But an urban transition is not a matter of simply matching problems to solutions; it needs complex and multi-faceted endeavours.

The crisis has shown us that the late 20th century agenda will be deeply problematic, because our urban metabolism is completely out of sync. So at the dawn of the 21st century we need a "smart metabolism": a powerful integrative and action-oriented body of thought on cities that emphasises their identities and their social composition, that analyses the resources it takes to run a city, that provides insights into intricate ways in which design, politics and business interrelate (Hajer and Dassen, 2014). The future calls for smart planning rather than smart cities.

THE SMART PLANNING PROTOCOL

The metabolism is a prerequisite for what we appreciate the cities as places of human improvement, creativity and exchange. We need to rethink the city so as to make it an environment, a configuration that is sustainable, socially just and resilient to future shocks. Smart Planning calls for a language that expresses more than efficiency and technology. We must defeat the idea of "smart cities from a box": generic concepts that are imposed on cities will not work. Several experimental green cities worldwide stand witness to what happens if we opt for sustainability, resilience and intelligence but continue following the planning concepts of the 20th century. Urban innovations (spatial, social, economic) are needed as much as technological ones, in order to achieve a more sustainable urban metabolism. In the end, it is most likely that an intelligent sum of social innovations, new technologies, new settlement models and new business models will provide the disruptive force needed to change the dominant modern "dummy" system.

To fight the challenge of a paradigm shift from the smart city to the smart planning in 2013 was set up in **Palermo** the **Smart Planning Lab**, a laboratory that integrates applied research, communication and education as part of i-NEXT Project (*Innovation for greeN Energy and eXchange in Transportation*), funded by the Italian Operative Program "Research and Competitiveness". It carries out three main functions: 1) as a producer of context and scenario analysis, and as a producer of solutions aimed at a new and more efficient regulation of life-cycles and the efficient localization of attractive urban functions (civic, cultural, economic and social); 2) as intelligent hub that allows a constant connection with the needs of urban planning and management, using sectorial analysis, crowdsourced informations or operational proposals and developing guidelines about good governance and integrated planning for sustainable development; 3) being permanent tool of communication and dissemination of methods and outcomes of the urban smartness.

The Smart Planning Lab integrates new digital technologies and methodologies, such as conceptual maps and crowdsourcing knowledge, with the Living Lab methodology to help creating and strengthening existing ties and resolve strategic issues in the real life of the cities.

The Smart Planning Lab, therefore, is an activator of education and training functions for public administrations in the processes of creative, smart and green urban regeneration.
It develops ICT services for digital citizenship for increasing the participation and sharing in green and smart oriented development programs. Finally, it produces information and dissemination for the growth of smart citizenship and social innovation. One of the first experiments in a *urban Operative System* was developed by Smart Planning Lab of the University of Palermo (Carta, 2014b) as a protocol for advanced planning to provide decision-makers, planners, managers and citizens of different multilevel urban instruments, able to rethink, redesign and live fully the smart city of the fifth generation, a smart city able to generate new social values and new economic value.

The **Smart Planning Protocol** (**Diagram n. 3**) is capable of interacting domain of governance and planning with that of the delivery of services. The protocol leads more sentient, intelligent and dialogue planning, capable of interacting with the objectives of innovation, competitiveness and cohesion pursued by social, civic and economic actors. The protocol works on the **decision-making processes** and **local development strategies** through processes of cloud governance and open urbanism. The inputs from the urban actors — sensors and actuators — are processed through the different instruments of integrated and strategic planning to be converted in outputs such as **smart tools**, **city apps** and **civic dashboards** for effective management of several urban fields and life cycles, as well as for an effective response to the needs of the community (policy-making, regulations, taxation, family services, mobility, building maintenance, environmental quality, innovation, housing, urban management, spatial planning). According to the protocol all output must be structured and calibrated according to the different levels of governance and action: from regional dimension (> 500 Km), through metropolis (100 Km) and city (10 Km) to district (1 Km). Each level needs specific urban smart devices and dashboards to improve the collective intelligence for starting a deep innovation.

The development and diffusion of smart technologies applied to spatial planning are leading to the experimentation of new interfaces with local territorial entities at different scales. In particular, on the Palermo metropolitan area is conducting a trial of methods of urban/human mapping and social communication that can enrich traditional systems to expand the possibilities for the use of geo-data in planning process, changing the way we collect, share and manage urban data. Thus, the planning process is modified through new ways of reading and interpreting macro-regions, strategic platforms, local systems and socio-economic relations, revealing connections still concealed that could lead to a non-institutional – but factual – redefinition of the metropolitan aggregations.
Today, we need to think about urbanism and planning from a global perspective. The task of the century may be to bring back the ideal of cities as place of exchange, inspiration, social mobility, enhanced quality of life, inclusion and reconnectedness to nature. If the modernist city was the city of the rational blueprint: survey, analysis, plan, the intelligent cities of the 21st century cannot work with this model.
Given the challenges cities face, we now need cities that can adapt, correct, adopt, and add on to existing practices and knowledge. A creative co-opetition requires citizens to stage and share successes and invites cities to excel.
The future of our more intelligent cities is the "project of all projects", and smart planning would create the conditions for continuous learning, reflection and adjustment, in oder to improve the urban condition for its inhabitants. And the only way to do that is to be open and share experiences and solutions.

THE URBAN REVOLUTION OF SELF-DRIVING CARS

The sentient city, the massive expansion of open data and dissemination of geo-information arising from the huge amount of data that comes from the multitude of sensors placed in the cities and from the community-based traffic and navigation apps (like Waze), engages in disruptive manner on the city's capabilities, on the use of services and spaces, on the environment and mobility management. And it is mobility that can take massive advantage from the extraordinary urban intelligence produced by diffusion and interconnection of sensors. In the coming years the city will have to manage innovation and the increase of intelligence produced by the introduction of a new component, apparently technological but in essentially related to urbanism: the driverless car. Autonomous systems are at various stages of maturity all over the world. In **Copenhagen's** metro the trains are driver-free and the system is run by a fully automated computer, which analyzes terabytes of data in real time and makes decisions based on it. And specific train lines in Paris, Vancouver, Sao Paulo, Barcelona, London, Singapore, Tokyo and Seoul also run (at least partially) autonomously. This is not just a technological innovation related to infrastructure and mobility model, but a different way of living in urban spaces modified by the use of intelligent cars constantly connected with the network of data, information and assessments within which cities will be more and more immersed.

According with the international survey conducted by Boston Consulting Group and the World Economic Forum about the relationship between diffusion driverless car, urban design and mobility practices - self-driving vehicles, robot-taxi and the urban mobility revolution — 58% of consumers surveyed say they would like a ride in a car without a driver. In Gothenburg, Sweden, in the coming months Volvo will drive 100 standalone machines to ordinary citizens: the biggest test in the world of self-driving car on public roads. Meanwhile, the European Union has launched Autocits Project to facilitate the spread of driverless vehicles in urban centers. Testing will take place on roads open to traffic in **Madrid**, **Paris** and **Lisbon**. We have to pass from the traditional Transit-oriented Planning (son of the previous mobility paradigm) to a more innovative intelligent and collaborative mobility ecosystem. The use of the Cooperative Intelligent Transport Systems (C-ITS) allows vehicles to communicate with other vehicles, with traffic signals and roadside infrastructure as well as with other road users and the huge amount of big data released everyday by smart citizens. With alerts generated from the increased information available, these systems have a strong potential to improve not only the road safety and the efficiency of the road transport, but also the urban management by a permanent interface among data. Thanks to the spread of autonomous robotic car with a driver and an urban mobility system developed around them, it would be enough for 30% of vehicles on the road today to cover a great city mobility needs. And this number could be reduced by a further 40%, if people were ready to share their journeys. The alliance of self-driving and shared cars (Uber, Bla Bla, Car2Go and their friends) could reduce by 90% the number of vehicles in circulation.

Cities, receiving a dividend of public space freed from cars, could reshape themselves passing from the era of the automobile toward the era of people mobility, turning secondary streets into citizen spaces for culture, leisure and the community. It's a deep paradigm shift – like as a return to basics – where smart planning must design and manage this dividend of spaces redistributing it in favor of lightweight personal mobility and more sustainable collective and sharing mobility. Augmented cities in the age of self-driving urbanism must plan and design trees instead of parking, manage cleaner air and fewer accidents. Driverless cars ask to reimagine the urban spaces, the location of services, the setting of districts, the housing facilities. Self-driving vehicles will become more and more personal and tailored to the needs of a "granular mobility" that significantly reduces occupied urban space (Gita, for instance, is an intelligent and nimble cargo vehicle designed and engineered by Piaggio Fast Forward as a personal pedestrian mobility assistance, imagined for the humans). One of the most impressive experiment in using the space dividend produced by mobility revolution is the Urban Mobility Plan of **Barcelona**, which promises a pathway to greener, cleaner, and more pedestrian-friendly urban living. The strategy is based around the concept of the "superilles" (superblocks): a mini-neighborhood created on a grid that confines higher-speed motorized traffic on the perimeter so that the interior roads are freed up for pedestrian-friendly public space. This simple yet smart retrofit of Barcelona's existing gridded neighborhoods is already underway and is part of a larger plan to reduce traffic by 21 percent over the next two years.

THE CITY OF SHARING KNOWLEDGE

01 SMART LAND PARADIGM
A Mediterranean way to a more intelligent urban/rural territory

from **Smart City**
the city that works actively to improve the quality of life of its citizens

to **Smart Land**
a territory sustainable, smart and inclusive as enabling platform for creativity and innovation

01. We live in an increasingly urbanized world with a powerful magnetization toward metropolis increasingly intelligent and creative. Emerge, however, often opposed – and even more often in complementary – new lifestyles of the urban / rural interpreted by the recent vitality of rural villages. Mediterranean Europe is proposed as a new paradigm capable of descrambling the conflict between a city more and more technological and more rural surroundings on a human scale, among the most attractive cities and rural villages that are depopulated. An urban environment more complex, made up of intelligence and resilience, competitiveness and cohesion in a position to take positive action to improve the quality of life of citizens who live there. This is the meaning of the **Smart Land** (theorized by Aldo Bonomi and Roberto Masiero), a larger area of the single dense city that comes to include rural areas, a more widespread area where cities and countries come together in a single intelligent territory, not only from a technological point of view, but also social, for cities – metropolitan, medium and small – more liveable and socially inclusive and able to promote the welfare of citizens. The Smart Land is therefore an urban / rural area in which to experience widespread and shared policies aimed at increasing the competitiveness and attractiveness of the territory with specific attention to social cohesion, innovation, dissemination of knowledge, creativity, accessibility and freedom of movement, to the usability of the environment and the quality of the landscape and the lives of citizens. The concept of Smart Land is not only an expansion of the smart city, but it is a new model that involves local actors, institutional, economic, cultural and social, to act in new ways on the landscape, cultural heritage, on manufacturing, on styles life and environmental sustainability.

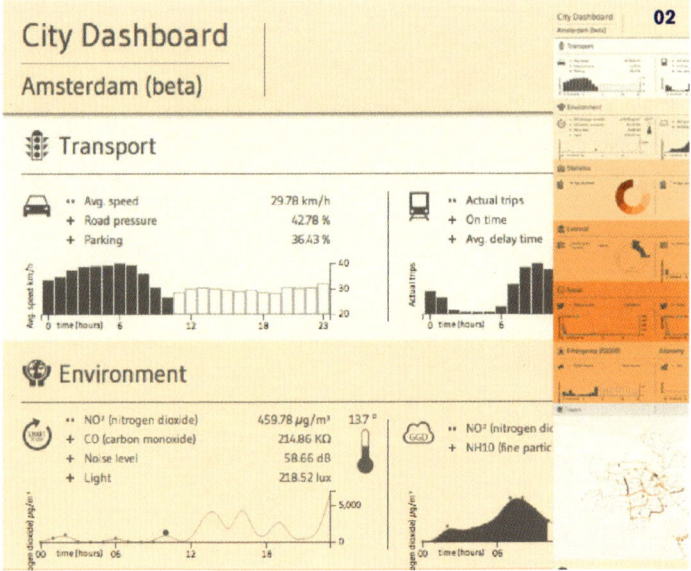

02. Amsterdam City Dashboard is a platform that shows what's happening in Amsterdam in every moment. Citizens and government agencies collect a lot of data, which they are opening up for public use more and more frequently. The dashboard makes use of the latest open data from a wide range of municipal services.

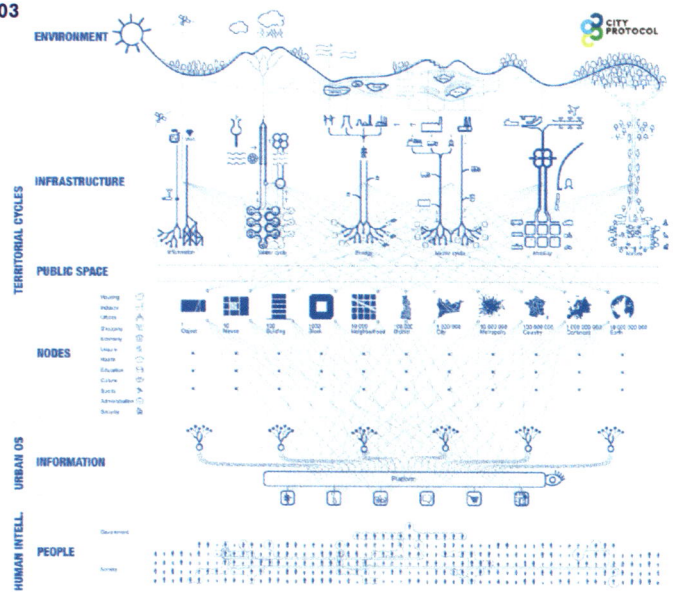

03. On March 1, 2012, the Mayor of Barcelona and the CEO of Cisco announced the "**City Protocol**", an agreement to launch a number of strategic initiatives aimed at advancing the city's objective of being a global reference model for sustainable urban development. The plan calls for creating blocks where consumers' energy needs are analyzed and compared with available alternatives in order to improve efficiencies. Another aim of the plan is to develop an energy use map for all of Barcelona based on these newly renovated blocks. To kickstart the program, the city government allocated two empty blocks in two different districts, Nou Barris and Sant Marti. The second one is situated within the 22@Barcelona technology district, a 200-hectare planned "city within a city" focused on bringing together companies, research facilities, training centers, and other elements of a technology hub.

04. On the quay of Barcelona was built the **Fab@House**, created by Fab Lab Barcelona with the assistance of Fab Lab MIT. It isn't a simply static construction, but a basis lay of a dynamic model, depending on geographical layout of the house. Its form changes to optimize allocation of heat inside and time of hit of the sun for solar batteries. This house completely provided itself with the electric power, even in the winter, and even allowed to sell excess of the electric power reversely in a network.

05. Pere IV is located in the heart of 22@ that intends to transform Poble Nou into the new area of social, urban and technological innovation in Barcelona. However, due to its historical condition as the old industrial zone, more than 32% of its area – buildings, lots and urban space – is unoccupied. This situation not only reflects a sense of abandonment of the public space but transcends to the lack of activity over time. It presents a void in space,

PERE IV
SMART STREET HOTEL

Alejandra Díaz de León / Dulce Luna / Priyanka Narula / Drew Carson

type and time. In order to re-activate the public space, we propose the street as a **Smart Street Hotel** that offers programmatic flexibility, spatial temporality and social/technological inclusion. It focuses on the current users interested in the area – researchers, designers, entrepreneurs, artist – and the future needs of these users as citizens. As new citizens of the world we have lost the sense of ownership and have become more interested in collecting experiences. That is why – through a booking system – we offer the possibility they can rent and design a space to perform and kind of activity as long as needed. As part of the booking system, users can observe augmented reality in their personal devices or tablets to interact with the urban space, find out about other users or friends, know which spaces are available or where events are happening in real time as they walk along the street.

06.a

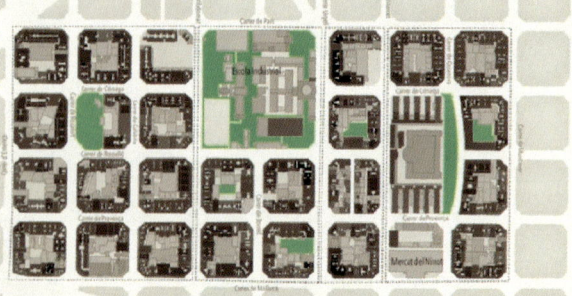

RESUM DE DADES

Superilles opció A
Districte de l'Eixample
Barris de La Nova Esquerra i Antiga Esquerra de l'Eixample

06. Superilles is one of the most impressive experiment in using the space dividend produced by mobility revolution. It's a part of the Urban Mobility Plan of Barcelona, which promises a pathway to greener, cleaner, and more pedestrian-friendly urban living. The strategy is based around the concept of the superblocks as a mini-district created on a grid that confines higher-speed motorized traffic on the perimeter so that the interior roads are freed up for pedestrian-friendly public space.

07.a

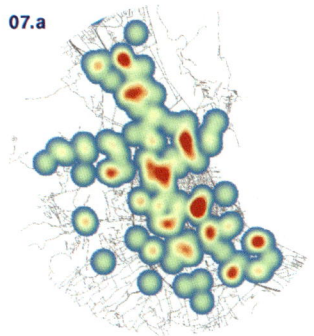 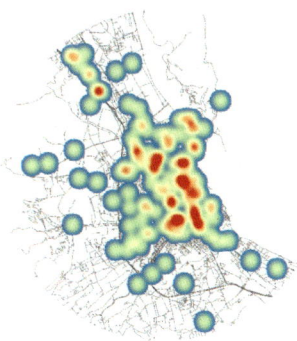

07. The smart city must adopt a model of planning/management of urban life cycles that is able to consistently integrate the ICT components with those of governance and the decisions about the location of main urban functions. In this field works the Smart Planning Lab (SPL), an applied research laboratory in advanced planning for smarter cities and social innovation, based at the University of Palermo. The SPL by integrating traditional sources of information and new forms of data produced by the fixed flow of communications, produces spatial analyses oriented towards urban planning oriented. With the use of specific algorithms and the interpretation of spatial information about mobility, energy and localization of urban functions, Smart Planning Lab analyzes urban metabolism with a new approach. The approach is innovative because it allows to analyze urban life with the help of energy and mobility data, social networks and databases (open data, big data, human data, etc). This approach is able to create an advanced urbanism whose city project is an ongoing and participatory process, capable of actively responding to several urban problems, including mobility and energy issues. The **Heat Map of Palermo** (above) renders the distribution and polarization direction of administrative services, public utilities and services at the neighborhood level through the use of an algorithm concentration "Heat Map". The representation, in variable shading, highlights with the warm tones the high concentration of services from their spatial distribution.
The **Lightness Map** (next page) displays classes of electricity consumption in the municipality. This map shows parts of the city according to energy sustainability, and indirectly monitors land usage, highlighting high residential concentrations, polarizations of services, and corresponding need for electricity supply (security), as well as energy waste.

07.c

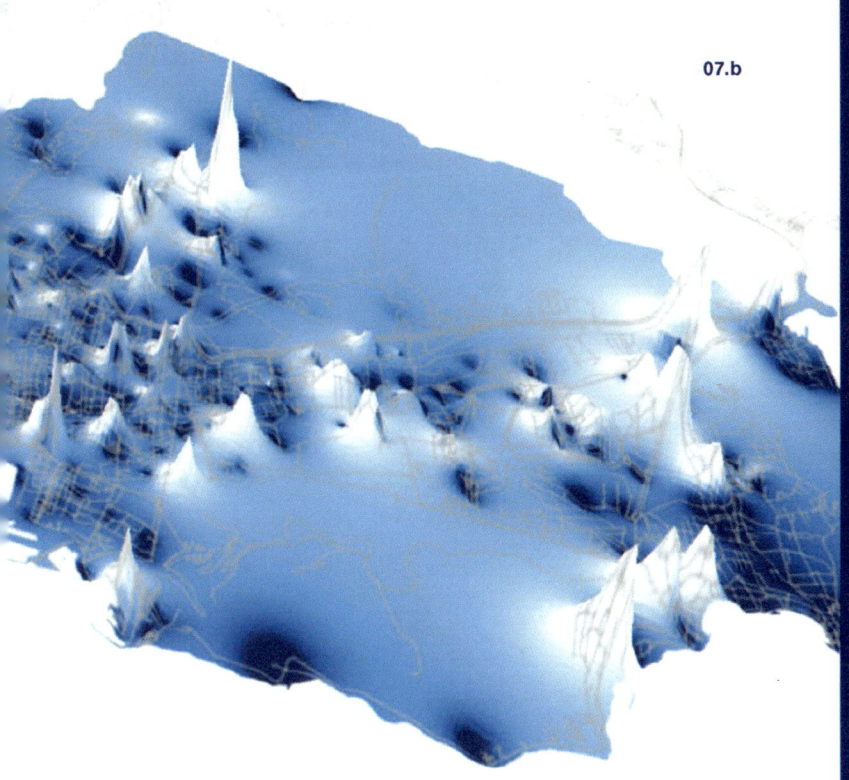

07.b

Bright areas (white) and less bright ones (blue) are shown in a 3D view in which the height corresponds to the absolute value of consumption. The **Hexagon Map** (left) shows the energy consumption of the municipal buildings and of the public lighting (each hexagon is a cluster of average consumption more than 10,000 KWh).

08. One of the most important research field of the Smart Planning Lab is about the spatial planning by human/urban data, able to represent in real time the everyday life of the inhabitants. The **Map of distribution of Social Networks Activity** allows to understand the people activity in urban spaces better than by traditional data. The hourly distribution of twitter activity in time bands is displayed through a Heat Map concentration algorithm that shows the streaming of twitter-originated human data. The Twitter social network has been chosen for its peculiarities in providing textual, spatial and temporal information, useful for analyzing home/work and/or free time, in real time. The map of social activity allows a real-time representation of the life of the city through the representation of the distribution of the people in order to effectively guide decisions relating to transport, the location of services and security. The location of this information is useful in monitoring the dynamics of use of the city: not from a static supply service point of view, but dynamically. This is helpful towards a sustainable and effective management of service delivery, mobility or energy management.

Smart Planning Protocol gains considerable benefit from the urban mapping produced through open and big data related to citizens. In particular, the connection with the intelligent applications that manage the transport, energy, water and waste can produce significant improvements in urban management, with increased efficiency and cost reduction.

HUMAN/URBAN DATA
PLANNING BY SOCIAL ACTIVITY

PALERMO twitter activity

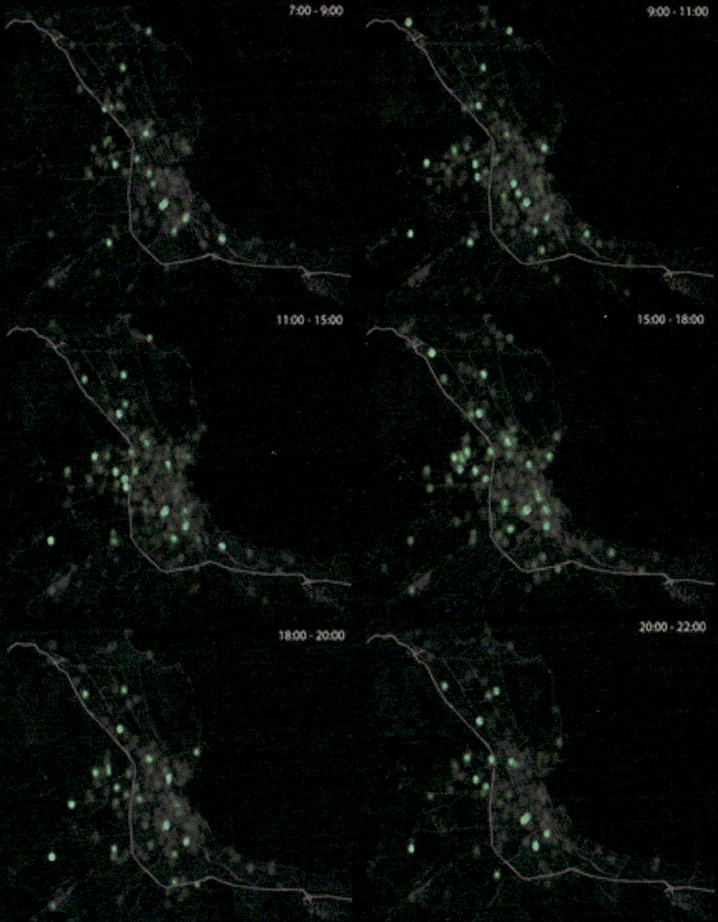

7:00 - 9:00 | 9:00 - 11:00
11:00 - 15:00 | 15:00 - 18:00
18:00 - 20:00 | 20:00 - 22:00

The next ten years will see a re-emergence of artisans as an economic force, but it'll be a new form of craftsman: the urban artisan. Like their medieval predecessors in pre-industrial Europe and Asia, these next-generation makers will play their trade outside the walls of big business, making a living with their craftsmanship and knowledge inside new fab cities.

4. PRODUCTIVE

THE FAB CITY
Creative/productive urban ecosystem

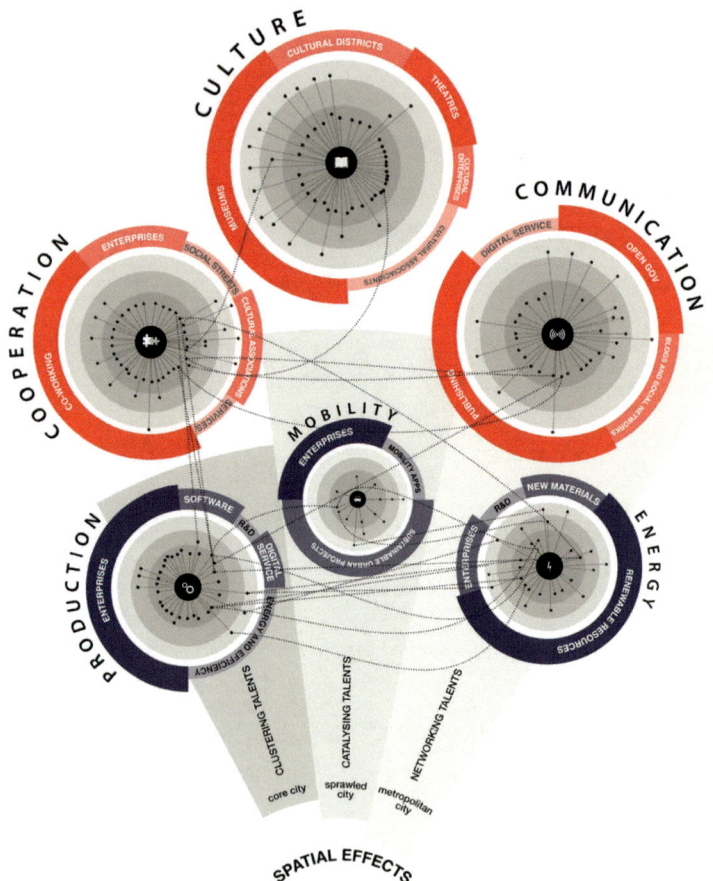

THE THIRD MANUFACTURING REVOLUTION

In the Great Global Crisis, especially in Europe, governments are committed to find new ways to restart up, even though some of them aim at correcting mechanisms within the same development model, thus risking to remake the same mistakes that led to the crisis. Other paths stem from the awareness that we are not merely faced with a temporary crisis but rather with a real metamorphosis of visions, paradigms and development protocols, and even of ecological, cultural, political, economic and social systems.

The Greek etymology of the word reminds us that the crisis involves recognition, hence "decision": it requires active identification and assessment that is the prerequisite to the necessary structural change. Nothing can remain unchanged and we have an obligation to rethink the identity and role played by the components of society as a whole, and how they affect urban and land planning. Naturally, the metamorphosis is neither a linear process nor is it exclusively rational and unidirectional, but feeds on circular paths, progresses and retrogressions, logic and empathy, affecting ethics and aesthetics. Therefore, the quality of cities being high on the agenda again seems to be one of the most effective solutions to reactivate evolutionary mechanisms. Strengthening an integrated vision with respect to urban design, started in the Nineties by EU Urban Program and then blocked by the real estate bubble – becomes an increasingly urgent opportunity to redefine competitiveness, quality and prosperity of the nations that have been hit by the tsunami of the crisis. The development metamorphosis paradigm requires capitalism to be re-imagined not only in terms of a more democratic dimension with different priorities, standards and values, but especially regarding a greater territorialization and a return to development policies based on territorial capitals, cities above all. The intertwinement between "territorial capitalism" (based on identity capitals) and "network capitalism" (based on flows capitals) will play a key role, between green and soft economy, legacy and innovation. Rethinking of the development model ought to be coupled with a new deal for urban planning, whose para-

digms, protocols and tools are to be renewed and reassessed so that they can go back to being essential for development instead of subjected to economy or emergency management.
In the Third Industrial Revolution is emerging a new figure of production: the community-driven company, successfully described by Chris Anderson as the future of the the long term business model with a constant trend to innovation and sharing. It's a company based on mutual aid, sharing objectives and risk mitigation through an equal distribution of responsibilities. A renewed Adriano Olivetti's company model that requires an adequate urban context because it is competitive with the traditional model. A new working class hero is emerging: the urban artisan. In according with Larry Katz, economist at Harvard University, the future "good" middle-class jobs will come from the re-emergence of artisans, or highly skilled people in each field. The next ten years will see a re-emergence of artisans as an economic force, but it'll be a new form of craftsman: the urban artisan. Like their medieval predecessors in pre-industrial Europe and Asia, these next-generation artisans will ply their trade outside the walls of big business, making a living with their craftsmanship and knowledge. But there also will be marked differences. In many cases, brain will blend with brawn as software and technology replace hard iron and hard labor. Urban artisans will call for a new urban ecosystem where they will craft not only their goods, but shape the economy with an effect reaching far beyond their neighborhoods, even their nations.

THE AGE OF URBAN INNOVATORS AND MAKERS

In 1934 Albert Einstein wrote "Insanity: doing the same thing over and over again and expecting different results. The crisis can be a great blessing for peoples and the nations as it brings about progress. Creativity is born from anguish, just like the day is born from the dark night", recognizing that it's in crisis that inventive is born, as well as discoveries and big strategies. The real crisis is the incompetence facing the challenge to find innovative solutions, risking to choose the routine option, a repeating action, continuing on a comfortable path that has been already marked: the symptom of a slow agony. If it is true that "without a crisis, any wind becomes a tender touch", the ability to navigate the stormy waters and to govern the winds that are sweeping global economies away, requires hard work and strong resolve.

The development model deformed by global finance and deficitary public spending has hidden the true capacity of territories, eroding resources, reducing opportunities and destroying the capability to compete on one's own merits. Political strategies and urban plans have been replaced by the developing agents that have focused resources on often ineffective interventions, based on the rhetoric of local development rather than on real assets of innovation and powerful visions, on quality projects and on the skill to generate future. Any pernicious " technocratic morphine" shall be definitely abandoned rejecting the comforting ideology of some kind of procedural adjustment or liberalization: the productive and social tissue's destiny must radically change, laying its foundations on the concepts of "limit", "environment" and "creativity". And it is especially in the urban field that the battle is to be fought, rethinking the role of the city as engine of territorial cohesion, as activator of collective intelligences, as catalyst of tangible and intangible assets and as *milieux innovateurs:* cities that feel and think.

New challenges await planners, local administrators, actors and regulators today, to effectively contrast the slowdown of the city's generating and driving capacity. After more than a century of Fordist industrial society – marked by excessive reliance on rationality – we shall enter the third industrial revolution age, which is not only characterized by the primacy of information and communication technologies, network access and the "internet of things" in which everything is connected on cloud.

In the third industrial revolution, as a matter of fact, passions shall be recovered as our decisions can be led by emotions as a complement to rational arguments In the metamorphosis era, the decisions taken within the realm of territorial development should be able to draw from the emotional impulses produced by opinions, attitudes, collective and individual beliefs and feelings. The coming decade will see continuing economic transformation of our cities and the emergence of a new artisan economy. Many of the new artisans will be small and personal businesses/merchant/craftspeople producing one of a kind or limited runs of specialty goods for an increasingly large pool of customers seeking unique, customized, or niche products. Only if these businesses will can rise from a new urban creative ecosystem they will attract and retain craftspeople, artists, and engineers looking for the opportunity to build and create new products and markets, before, and a more productive city, after.

FROM FAB LAB TO FAB CITY

In a renewed empathetic approach, the metamorphosis of the territorial management is likely to find that the urban armature of developing areas — Southern Europe above all — provides an important experimental field as it is no longer just a matter of raw materials, land to be consumed, low-cost manufacture and consumers, but socio-cultural inclusiveness, forward-looking vision. Moreover, it is fundamental to place Mediterranean Europe at the centre, which will have to intercept the re-establishment of powers and leadership. Europe is witnessing the end of a historical cycle. Globalization has entered the redistribution stage of economic dynamics, wealth and power between the West and the emerging markets. This change means that many Western and European countries are being forced to reassess their models without being able to resort to formulas that are suitable for times of growth and prosperity. The budgetary stringency is associated with the temptation of a liberalization which can, in turn, lead to deregulation in the allempt to provide economy with the necessary room to restart the system. But times have changed: the ecological crisis, the scarcity of raw materials, the pre-default of the sovereign debt and the reduction of consumption can no longer be ignored. At this stage, the consumerist and dissipative model linked with the exploitation of land resources to guarantee our well-being is not an option. In order not to completely abandon the welfare state, the way we inhabit the planet shall be reinvented, in the pursuit of a development model able to reconnect material resources in a productive and reproductive mode. What we need is a territorial metabolism from consumption to production.

One of the most advanced experiments in FabLab-based production model is the **Valldaura Labs** in the metropolitan area of **Barcelona**. It is a project promoted by IaaC (Institute for Advanced Architecture of Catalonia) for the creation of a self-sufficient habitat research centre. Located in the Collserola Natural Park, it has laboratories for the production of energy, food and things, and develops projects and academic programmes in association with leading research centres around the world. Valldaura Green FabLab is an opportunity to learn directly from nature in order to bring that understanding to the regeneration of 21st-century cities.

To improve the makers' ecosystem the Municipality of Barcelona has launched in 2014 the **Fab City Initiative** to support communities and private initiatives in order to build a richer ecosystem around digital fabrication. The initiative will bring different communities – productive, technological, social and cultural – together and help to build the Fab City, which – says Tomas Diez, leader of Barcelona Fablab – is not one-side vision of the city as a laboratory, but a complete ecosystem which includes also industries, universities, commerce and many more civic and social actors which could benefit and participate of it. In a Fab City, citizens are empowered to be the leaders of their own destiny, their creativity is improved, their resilience is increased and a more ecological system is developed because movement of materials and energy consumption is drastically reduced.The Fab City Initiative will turn Barcelona in a creative/productive city in few years, bringing back productivity inside the city, to the citizens, to promote local innovation connected to a global network, to re-industrialize the city, and to produce value on top of that, which will affect every single aspect of the life of people.

In the track of Barcelona, **Palermo** has edited a "Map of Talents, Creativity and Innovation", identifying all the places dedicated to creativity and innovation in order to understand the logic of the settlements of new fab city's makers. The map is useful to identify the existence of emergent creative clusters but especially, in our proactive vision, is useful to guide future planning decisions towards the creation of a spatial ecosystem that facilitates the rise, development and profitability of the city of innovative production (tangible and intangible). The map was edited led by a conceptual scheme (**Diagram n. 4**) that describes the spatial, economic and social implications. The Fab City as productive ecosystem is divided in the two macro-sectors of **creativity** and **innovation**, considered as main productive domains of talents's skills. The first sector is articulated in **cultural** places (museums, theaters, etc.), **communication** activities (publishing, open gov, digital services, etc.) and **cooperation** spaces (social streets, co-working, etc.). Innovation is divided into places related to digital **manufacturing**, sustainable **mobility** and renewable **energy**. For understanding the factors to "augment" the productive city, it's necessary to identify the relationships among the different spheres of activities (among places and subjects both), in order to understand the network of relationships that could generate the ecosystem. The productive city as fab city network produce its spatial effects on three levels that identify the productive metabolism for diversifying the diagnosis and subsequent action: a) the **core city**, the dense city in which innovative production acts as a *clustering* tool for the utilities and for the self-sufficiency of housing; b) the **sprawled city**, the dispersed city in which the creative and innovative production acts as a densifier of places and flows, and the talents become potential *catalysts* for new settlement and regeneration; c) the **metropolitan city**, the city-region where production is integrated with the return of manufacturing and peri-urban agriculture, with tourism and with the rethinking of energy model; at this scale creative and innovative talents act more like connectors for *networking* of activities.
The Fab City involves civic leaders, makers, urbanists and innovators

working on changing the paradigm of the current industrial economy. The Palermo Map of Talents want be able to act on the urban policy with the principles of the circular economy, which supplies not only the Third Industrial Revolution of the makers, but also a social — and hence urban — revolution based on re-cycling. Recycling economies, in fact, show how marginal economies are producing new social collectives and projects around local and global decay, often with waste labor bringing high monetary reward as well as danger (Alexander and Reno, 2012). Recently William McDonough (2013) raised the concept of "upcycling", insisting on the need to create an industry — but we add a city — that creates value and that is not limited simply to not be harmful or dissipative. The Ellen MacArthur Foundation has extended the approach of circular economy in early innovation processes of industrial regeneration, such as the Renault factory in **Choisy-le-Roi** (Paris area). This factory is specialised in the remanufacture and recycling of automotive parts, allowing substantial savings to be made in terms of raw materials. In U.S. are raising several re-manufacturing cities led and supported by federal government and makers movement initiatives both. Among these one with more start-up appeal is **Nashville**, which, renowned as creative scene for its music scene, is becoming a centre for makers. These activities are regenerating several districts without gentrify them, transforming the city in a vibrant new creative/productive hub.

Fab City is the great challenge of the mature phase of makers movement. It is a new urban model of transforming and shaping cities that shifts how they source and use materials and data in a in-out process. A Fab City is a new urban model for locally productive and globally connected self-sufficient cities.

CITY AS PRODUCTIVE ECOSYSTEM

01-02. In 2014 the Municipality of Barcelona has launched the ambitious project "Fab Cities". With this project the city of Barcelona wants to support the birth of a network of nearby FabLab and, within six years, the foundation of a laboratory in each district of the town that is active and integrated with local communities and urban policies. In the same cultural line, the *Smart Planning Lab* of the University of Palermo has launched the **Map of Talents, Creativity and Innovation**, which identifies in Palermo all places dedicated to creativity and innovation, in order to understand the logic of settlements – spontaneous today – of the new urban makers, but especially to guide future planning decisions towards the formation of a creative ecosystem that facilitates the startup, development and profitability of the city's innovative production. The map identified and located more than 250 "places of talent", divided between the two macro-areas of creativity and innovation. The macro area of creativity was located in cultural places (museums, theaters, etc.), communication activities (publishing, open gov, digital services, etc.) and cooperation areas (social Streets, co-working, etc.). The innovation macro-area has been identified in places related to digital production, sustainable mobility and renewable energy. Among the various areas of activity has been identified the possible relationship between sites or between subjects, in order to understand the network of connections and flows that make up the ecosystem. Besides mapping the places/activities, a cluster analysis was made, allowing the display of the concentrations and distributions of places by categories. This identifies "epicenters of creativity and innovation" of the city, so as to better understand the current logic of location, but especially the future incentivize logic. The data were also aggregated and presented in a visual form to allow a quick understanding of the mutual relations between places and activities, the current collaborations and the "ecosystem trials" that can be identified today.

The **Map of Talents** is now starting to provide an interesting clustering of the city and provides a view of the forms of spontaneous aggregation which should be favoured, facilitated or re-oriented to be more effective. Then it wants to be a first contribution to build the network of Fab City, able to operate in an urban policy following the principles of circular economy. In this way, not only the Third Industrial Revolution of the producers is supported, but also the social urban revolution based on recycling. The new philosophy of re-cycling shows how the marginal cost economies are producing new collective projects and new forms of sociality opposing the local and global decline.

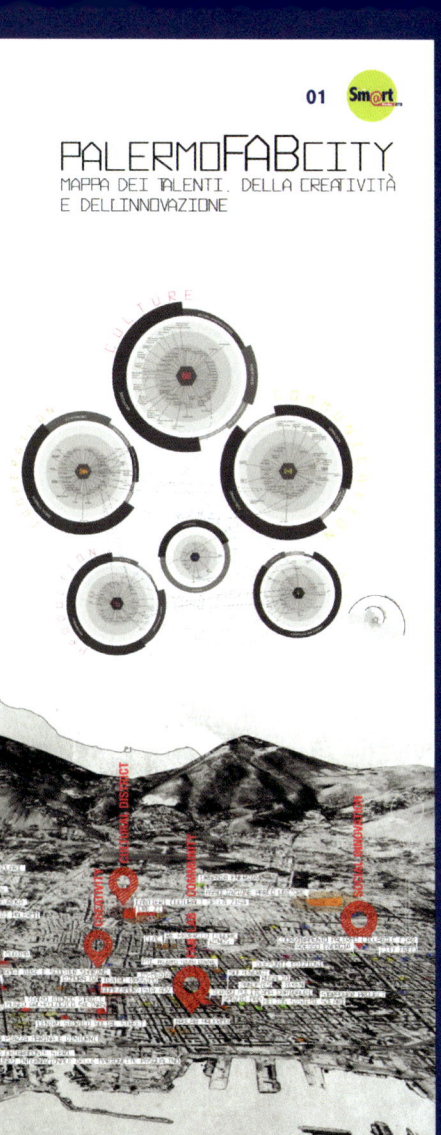

PALERMOFABCITY
MAPPA DEI TALENTI, DELLA CREATIVITÀ E DELL'INNOVAZIONE

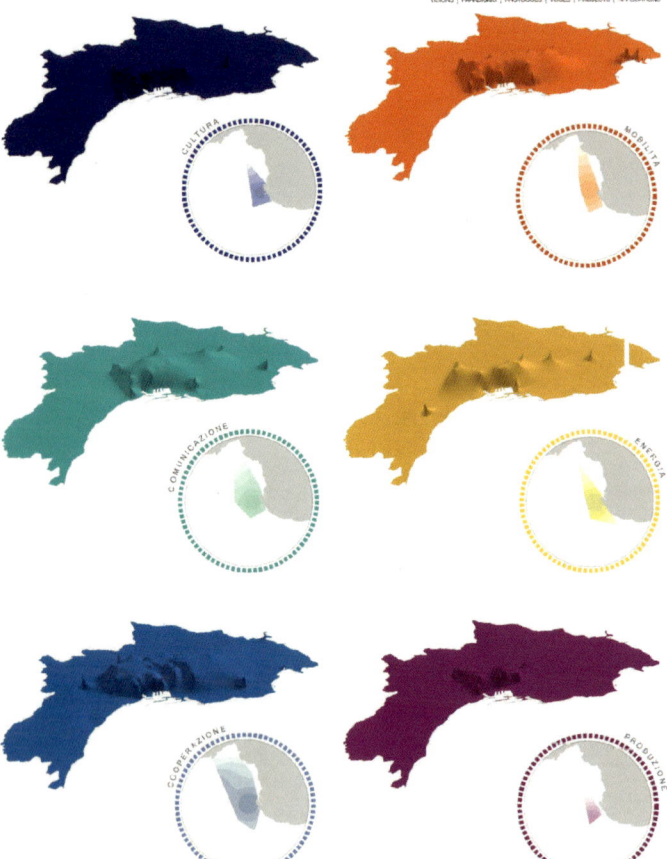

03. San Diego's Makers Quarter begins with what matters most: community. The promoters are collaborating with community partners to create change in an area that has been void for years. With thought, vision and innovation we are transforming Makers Quarter into a neighborhood San Diegans can be proud of. We believe when looking to the future, it is best to start by embracing the past while celebrating the present. San Diego's Makers Quarter is a live/work/play neighborhood that is more than just a new place. This is a melting pot where creative culture brings to life a collaborative community. It's a place that embraces the past while ushering in the future. Makers Quarter is the newest addition to San Diego's burgeoning and vibrant Downtown, which is home to nearly 75,000 employees and 35,000 residents in several distinctive and unique districts. These include the vibrant and evolving East Village, the historic Gaslamp Quarter, lively and scenic Little Italy, as well as shopping and dining in Horton Plaza and Seaport Village.

04. The **Fab Labs** are the new actors in urban scene. The Fab Lab program was initiated to broadly explore how the content of information relates to its physical representation and how an under-served community can be powered by technology at the grassroots level. The program began as a collaboration between the Grassroots Invention Group and the Center for Bits and Atoms at the Media Lab in the Massachusetts Institute of Technology. The Fab Lab model from Usa has found great success in Barcelona thanks to the academic relationships between MIT and IAAC. This Institute for advanced architecture has installed the first Fab Lab in Poblenou district as the first spark of regeneration.

05. 22@Barcelona project transforms two hundred hectares of industrial land of Poblenou into an innovative district offering modern spaces for the strategic concentration of intensive knowledge-based activities. This initiative is also a project of urban refurbishment and a new model of city providing a response to the challenges posed by the knowledge-based society. It is the most important project of urban transformation of Barcelona city of the last years and one of the most ambitious of Europe of these characteristics, with a high real state potential and a 180 million Euros public investment of infrastructure plan. 22@Barcelona project transforms the old industrial areas of Poblenou in a high-quality environment for working, living and learning. As a project of urban refurbishment, it responds to the necessity of recovering the social and economic dynamism of Poblenou and creates a diverse and balanced environment

where the different facilities coexist with state-subsidized buildings, equipments and green spaces that improve life and working quality. As a project of economic refurbishment, it constitutes a unique opportunity to turn Poblenou into an important scientific, technologic and cultural platform transforming Barcelona into one of the most dynamic and innovative cities throughout the world. As a project of social refurbishment, it facilitates the interrelation among different professionals who work in the area and the participation of the district's neighbours in the opportunities information technologies offer. In this creative scenario, in 2016 the Fab City Initiative has explored the Fab City as a new urban model of transforming and shaping cities that shifts how they source and use materials from "Products In Trash Out" (PITO) to "Data In Data Out" (DIDO). A city's imports and exports would mostly be found in the form of data (information, knowledge, design, code). The **Fab City Prototype** is based on three particular subjects that are key to designing a roadmap for the future of the Poblenou: a) Fabrication & materials: with complementary production ecosystems happening inside the local network of Fab Labs, citizens have the possibility to produce what they consume, recirculating materials inside the neighbourhood and the city to reduce waste and carbon emissions associated with long-distance mass production and distribution chains. b) Food production: growing food on the rooftops of Barcelona. Through urban agriculture practices, citizens can grow part of what they eat turning production of local clean food in a regular pat of their lives. c) Energy: Renewable energy production. With the arrival of domestic batteries and the cost drop of solar technologies, citizens have the tools to produce part of their domestic energy consumption.

06. Valldaura Labs is a project promoted by IaaC for the creation of a self-sufficient habitat research centre. Located in the Collserola Natural Park, in the heart of the metropolitan area of Barcelona, it has laboratories for the production of energy, food and things, and develops projects and academic programmes in association with leading research centres around the world. The group comprises three laboratories — Food Lab, Energy Lab and Green FabLab — which produce the three things we need to be self-sufficient: food, energy and many of the things essential to the good life, combining the age-old ancestral knowledge that connects us to nature with the latest advanced technology. The laboratories are geared to investigating the processes involved in the production of energy, food and things locally, using the resources of the immediate environment, and developing technologies and knowledge that can be employed in the construction of a new global human habitat. As part of the production cycle they have created the **Green FabLab**, a digital fabrication lab that uses natural resources and is a partner in the international network of FabLabs led by MIT in Boston, and part of the Plan Avanza national network of laboratories in Spain. One of our lines of research is centred on the development of new materials from natural ingredients such as wood, earth or minerals for building, to make bricks, glass and resins using simple ancestral technologies and modern high-tech processes. At Valldaura it's carried out the complete cycle of matter transformation, from a sustainably managed tree in the forest which gives wood that is dried, designed, and cut on machines running on renewable energy to produce furniture and structural elements

Urban areas undergoing transformation can catch up and implement the new architectural and social quality and liveability of public spaces provided they aspire to overcome the creative single-cluster logic promoting a more effective creative eco-system able to connect and extend the districts' influence in a polycentric and reticular view.

5. CREATIVE

THE CREATIVE LAND
Human creativity for active cities

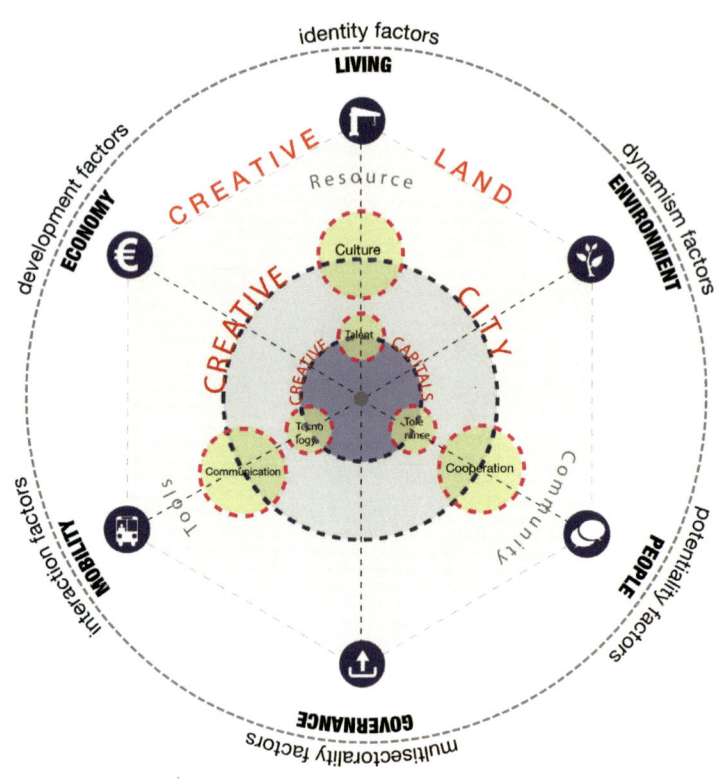

THE GENERATIVE CITY

Urban creativity is a hard challenge! It doesn't need rules or models, but protocols applicable in different local contexts, able to mount resources, capacity building and creative environments. The planning effort for the creative city requires not limiting to the identification of the creative milieu's general features (Florida and Tinagli, 2004) or the identification of operational universal tools (Landry, 2007). It challenges us to find local features that could provide good practices to be turned into methodologies or components to forge new urban regeneration tools, based on the cultural armature. Urban areas undergoing transformation and rural land in transition can catch up and implement the new architectural and social quality and liveability of public spaces provided they aspire to overcome the creative single-cluster logic promoting a more effective creative eco-system — a true creative land — able to connect and extend the districts' influence in a polycentric and reticular view.

Cities should rethink existing activities and identities (capitals and talents) through urban regeneration, rural development and districtualization strategies involving economic, social and infrastructure initiatives to implement innovative projects fuelled by the soft economy (Chapain et al., 2010) based on spatial quality, local excellence and the wide cultural armature of the territory. The current phase, focusing on tangible anti-crisis policies requires creative investments to be even more effective, losing too intangible or purely financial features to work within the local socio-economic context, hence the global one. Economy and urban policies can use the creative city's swing power to emerge from the quagmire of the crisis, plus creativity's added value, which optimises acceleration to be used as cultural growth machine given its ability to simultaneously influencing the overall size of the networks and the territorial local dimension, the tangible dimension of urban regeneration, the architectural heritage enhancement and the intangible dimension of cultural activities promotion and cultural heritage valorisation.

We live in a Creative Land composed by generative cities, a wide palimpsest of innovation labs, as experimented by several worldwide networks supporting what's variously termed social enterprise, community interest companies, impact economy, organizations that aim to create positive social impact through enterprise. By connecting members, co-working places, talent gardens, creative incubators, rural communities the Creative Land aims to create collaborative relationships between talented people who can turn thoughts into action when dealing with today's social, cultural and environmental issues. In the creative-based transition towards a permanent interaction among informations, innovation, education and research, also the university-city ecosystem must be enforced for acting as a more open, dialogic and connected source and as a power for urban regeneration, activating creativity and innovation, sharing knowledge and intelligence and educating to sustainable development. Building creative communities is one of the main topic of the new strategic agendas of universities for synchronising the development of the campuses with that of the cities in a more effective creative metabolism.

CREATIVE LAND GENOME

Culture could be most effective sustainable dimension of development (Unesco, 2015) if it's able to deeply interact with other dimensions, constituting their fertile base for developing. In this generative vision, creativity is an enabling device for culture-based sustainable development, and it can act as an "upgrader" for cities and communities in the Neo-Anthropocene.

Creativity is one of the most important component of the Augmented City's genome, defining its urban/human identity. The creative genome needs a fertile ecosystem — not just as an environment — for developing a powerful human settlement able to act as a generator of new cultural, social, economic and, above all, spatial relationships.

For interpreting and design the creative land we have to map its genome for understanding not only the components, but the opportunities and the operational actions. As showed in **Diagram n.5.** the creative land genome combines and interfaces the traditional creative capitals (**talent, technology and tolerance**) with creative chromosomes and their smart city's accelerators. The first interface agent is **Culture**, the territorial identity, steeped in history yet also extending into the future. Tangible and intangible culture is the most distinctive and competitive urban/rural resource, its identity and diversity as products of its history. Because the talent of a community could generate value, it must be submerged in the virtuous circle of the culture economy, the geography of experience, the design of quality. Culture, therefore, plays a part in the field of **Resources**, enabling cities to become more creative in the sectors of *living, economy* and *environment.*

The second generative factor of creative genome is **Communication**, namely a city's ability to inform, divulge information and involve in real time its citizens and multitude of users, using all kind of technology and making possible interventions aimed at cutting down congestion and deterioration: a city which makes effective use of innovation technology is, indeed, also one which cuts down on travelling, keeps a check on pollution and improves the way we work, delocalizing services and repositioning their centrality. Communication provides the setting of **Tools** for development acceleration in the fields of *economy, mobility* and *governance.*

And finally, the third creative factor is **Cooperation**, because, in global and multicultural cities, tolerance implies not merely the acceptance of other cultures and ethnic groups which remain at the margins of mainstream city life. The challenge faced by creative/generative land lies instead in the explicit collaboration among diversities, through cooperation among all users, between city centres and suburbs, between urban and rural functions. The creative land is not merely more open, multicultural and multiethnic, but it must be capable of mobilizing its diverse component parts in the pursuit of a plan for the future. Cooperation, therefore, redefines the **Community**, assigning it new roles and clearer objectives for empowering smarter people relationships with *governance* and *environment.*

We may identify three main stages of urban policies enabling to activate the creative ecosystems by connecting polycentric clusters, spreading the district effects and reducing the negative effect of the creative polarisation.

First, an effective urban policy must strengthen districts' competitiveness by adopting leverage strategies (identity, cultural resources, city branding) to be integrated with the metropolitan dimension increasing both its extension and scope, hence its power. Mobility and communication infrastructures shall therefore be strengthened, especially focusing on the large transnational networks (ports and airports), and the development of provision services for industries, especially high-added value innovative services promoting networking. The importance of interventions aimed at extending and strengthening human capital, skills and expertise available shall not be neglected, that focus on education and research as well as promoting interaction between actors within clusters and inter-cluster, including intermediary parties (agencies, joint ventures, advisor, etc.). Likewise, tax and financial incentives acting as a link with strong clusters in the sphere of creativity are of paramount importance, just as much as promoting new latent activities starting from the social capital in the less central areas.

The second stage relates to policies for the spreading of creative clusters effects in the entire human settlement within an ecosystem perspective. These are mainly aimed at reducing the environmental and energy impact, providing stimulus for the social accountability of established industries, by including rules for encouraging financial compensation of the fees for planning permission and the negotiated reallocation of part of the profits for urban quality interventions.

A more aware territorial planning project must lead and settle the activities and businesses within the creative ecosystem so as to reassess the generated flows, and above all to avoid possible congestion risks owing to new land and services demands.

Transferring the results of a successful creative cluster ought to focus on the overall image of the city, leveraging the brand for the purpose of strengthening credibility and the resulting attractiveness of investments, people and users, including flagship project as accreditation (Bilbao has set the standard in this sense). Naturally, how some of the best known urban projects will be redefined is unknown yet, because of the global economic crisis, but there is no doubt that in times of infrastructural and construction anti-crisis measures, a clear, comprehensive and consistent strategy facilitates the allocation of public resources in projects where a positive private business case already exists, retaining initial investments (Nantes, Marseille and Hamburg projects provide some empirical evidence).

Urban creativity has definitely exited from its intangible sector entering in urban sustainability policies, not only by affirming principles but demonstrating practices. The 116 cities of the **Unesco Creative Cities Network** call for placing creativity and cultural industries at the heart of urban development in support of economic, social, cultural and environmental sustainability, and actively cooperating at the international level. The creative-based Augmented Cities thus work at both the local and internationals levels, developing partnerships involving the public and private sectors, as well as civil society, and sharing best practices towards: strengthening the creation, production, distribution and dissemination of cultural activities, goods and services; developing hubs of creativity and innovation and broadening opportunities for creators and professionals in the cultural sector; improving access to and participation in cultural life, in particular for marginalized or vulnerable groups and individuals. And, overall, the cities must integrate culture and creativity into their sustainable development plans and processes.

The challenges faced by the creative cities include the need to transform derelict areas for contemporary urban uses, to enhance the inclusion of socially-marginalized groups, and to improve the dynamics and diversity of their urban economies. Creative cities are tackling these challenges, among others in a holistic approach, by instigating activities linked to their respective creative field and fully capitalizing on their creative assets as a basis for building sustainable, inclusive and balanced development in economic, cultural, environmental and social terms. Solutions include built interventions in the urban fabric, the organization of urban festivals and events fostering cultural participation, reinforcing the capacities of cultural professionals, training and supporting new talents, investigating new forms of creation and the adoption of policies and measures that support an enabling environment for local creative industries. Thus, by focusing their actions on human capital and local know-how, creative cities not only reinforce their inhabitants' sense of identity and pride, but also their capacity to generate new values, sources of income and social cohesion.

Augmented Cities based on creativity are hubs of innovation and breeding grounds for the development of new strategies, policies and initiatives aimed at making culture and creativity a driving force for sustainable development and urban regeneration, helping to increase opportunities for a broader range of communities, while contributing to more inclusive social patterns and urban economies.

In this way, creative cities respond to major local challenges such as the economic crisis, environmental degradation, demographic growth and social tensions, and can exchange experiences and best practices at the international level. They demonstrate that the creative assets play a vital role in sustaining local economies and in creating new economic opportunities. They help improve access to and participation in cultural life, as well as the enjoyment of cultural goods and services, particularly among marginalized or vulnerable groups and individuals. Moreover, the Unesco Creative Cities offers exceptional opportunities for cities to draw on peer learning processes and collaborative projects at the regional and international levels in order to foster the creativity inside the planning and management structure. "Human Cities: Challenging the City Scale", for instance, is a four year-long programme led by the Cité du Design in **Saint-Étienne** (France), implemented in the framework of Creative Europe 2020, which explores the reshaping of public spaces through design, with the overall objective of affirming the central role of creativity in the public policies and action plans of cities.

In the field of creativity-driven development, the synergy between universities and cities could activate concrete actions by setting up the transition of urbanity towards the "univer-city": city as an opensource laboratory of sustainable habitat oriented to creativity and innovation, and based on a close collaboration between universities, enterprises, institutions and local communities. Many case studies highlights how international cooperation between cities and universities has produced new sustainable settlements. To mention just some of them, in **Nantes**, the Quartier de la Création is based on the interaction between universities and enterprises by facilitating the forces of innovation and productivity. In the international consultation **Grand Paris** it has been outlined the establishment of an Université Libre as open, democratic and creative structure able to bring together all those invested in the construction of an urban strategy for the future of the metropolis, reinforcing the local presence of the university.

As for the third stage, it encompasses actions to reduce the negative effects of a creative cluster, either within the property market realm to contrast gentrification, which would level out the cultural and generational diversity, thus flattening creativity through compensation policies (rent control, reserve allowances for social housing, tax benefits for young couples etc.). Even the improvement of urban mobility through infrastructure planning and the promotion of intermodality and the proper management of public transport systems significantly contribute to avoid the burden of congestion and land use, other than strengthening the ecosystem view.

URBAN CREATIVITY AS SOCIAL CATALYST

The Augmented City could be seen as a spatial network of social catalysts. "Cities are living organisms: if they are not cultivated in the right way, they wither and die. The architecture has the power to place individuals in a community and to revive the forgotten corners of our urban fabric; communities use it to plant a flag and reunite", says Marc Kushner, founder of the online platform *Architizer*. In our creative-based vision social catalysts can be art galleries, youth centres, education buildings, creative incubators, shared spaces, libraries or museums: powerful urban tools to encourage the responsible action of the social body. Main challenge for advanced urbanism must be plan the urban rooting of these social catalysts and design the connection with other networks that shape the city.

Focusing on the social capital is essential not only regards improving the labour market's skills, but by promoting empowerment, thus encouraging self-employment and association networks, in order to facilitate the transition towards the creative economy.

The intense and strong ties between institutional actors and stakeholders involved in the creative ecosystem is a critical success factor, hence urban planners' need to encourage the emerging of such ties in terms of urban plans, projects, norms and conditions.
In this sense, the presence of places of proximity and relationship (urban center and living lab, community centres and incubators, co-housing and co-working) and the localisation of cultural, sport or leisure services act as social catalyst and it is an important prerequisite for strengthening the social capital among the different actors involved in the ecosystem. The Center for Social Innovation inaugurated in 2013 in **New York** is an example: 24 thousand sqm dedicated to offices (Diller and Scofidio have their), co-working, social enterprises incubation and NGOs in few years has encouraged the enhancement of social capital in the districts and the rooting of cultural networks already present in the area. In **Detroit**, Unesco Creative City of Design, the O.N.E. Mile project is dedicated to advancing the idea that creativity and design can be a catalyst for change, connecting context, program, and people. Starting in 2014

the project improves collaborative planning, cross-pollination of ideas, and consultation with the original members of Parliament Funkadelic, contributing to the idiosyncratic visual and cultural quality of the Oakland North End district.

It's in Southern Italy that we assist at a peculiar alliance between historical heritage and creative innovation, between identities and prospectives, producing several experiments of creative-based urban regeneration oriented to catalyse new social capital. **Matera's** Unmonastery Project is a community of young digital natives that share their skills with the community acting for its digital empowerment. The Re-action City Project and other projects by *Pensando Meridiano* in **Reggio Calabria** act as citizenship activator recycling disused areas, infrastructures and landscape for realising new community spaces. The knowledge atelier *ex Fadda* in **Puglia** is a public space for participation, creativity and social innovation with a strong orientation to economic self-sustainability. In the art-based regeneration initiative by *Periferica* in **Mazara del Vallo** a community of young urban professional share their skills with children, aged person and immigrants for building a new creative and multicultural community able to revitalise the declining historical centres of the towns.

The best Italian experiment ongoing of creative social catalyst – with an international reputation – is the **FARM Cultural Park** in **Favara**, a little town in Southern Sicily just 8 km from Agrigento's Unesco Archaeological Park "Valley of the Temples", but seven years ago it had never featured on any tourist map. Until now. Today FARM acts powerfully as a tornado in the current debate about how to make small communities survive global changes and economic crisis, and how to identify unused resources to make them an empowering instrument of sustainable growth and social innovation. The project was born in 2010 from the desire, passion and ability of the patron of the arts Andrea Bartoli (cultural agitator he says of himself) and his wife Florinda, who recycled an abandoned district turning it into a worldwide cultural centre devoted to contemporary arts, architecture, design and social innovation. The creative district, called "Sette Cortili" (seven courtyards), includes a breakthrough contemporary art museum, a residence for artists from around the world, an innovation-oriented co-working space, a space dedicated to an innovative School of Architecture for Children, a leisure garden – called "riad" as tribute at the Moroccan tradition – with a high stars hotel suite for art travellers, a bookshop, a concept store and several ethnic food spaces that mix Mediterranean culinary traditions. Exteriors of buildings are used as canvases for huge paintings and sculptures by young artists such as Fabio Melosu, Frabianco, Sara Fratini, Make and Analogique, courtyards feature permanent or temporary installations.

"FARM is a museum of people", says Andrea Bartoli to underline the community meaning of the successful experiment: not a cold fusion of art and city – like a lot of other gentrification-oriented practices – but a hot alliance among local community, regeneration space, private initiative, global art networks, creativity and identity.

The initiative, at its seventh year, has contributed to regenerate the entire old town of Favara with numerous shared urban design initiatives to return it to citizens and connect it with European counterparts through international cultural and tourism networks. Today the great ruin of the Cafisi Palace, ex scythes factory and then asylum in the center of town is reopened and made available by the young artists of Rudere Project, hosting exhibitions, literary events and temporary installations pending the launch of its complete restoration as part of a new interest of investors for Favara's real estate. Last FARM's challenge will be the realisation within five years, only by crowdfunding, of the first Children's Museum, restoring an old building near the district as a young empowerment machine for educating and nurturing a new "FARM generation" of creatives, innovators and changemakers, from South of the world to act in global arena. FARM is one of the best experiment of Cityforming Protocol (as explained in chapter 10 of this volume), because it has refused a masterplan approach, impossible to realise in that context, preferring a project-based incremental approach timed by colonisation, consolidation and development phases. In its first seven years FARM Cultural Park has acted as a creative colony for forming an adequate ecosystem and a sufficient cultural atmosphere for farming a true community of visionaries and innovators, designer and artisans, dreamers and entrepreneurs able to consolidate the initial local experiment for further development and propagation to entire town. The effect was the reactivation of the entire cultural system of Favara through a new attractiveness of the small Sicilian town for the worldwide creative class and through emulation by other initiatives that feed the FARM's brand.

FARM is not only an effective renewal of houses, public spaces and streets that form the seven courtyards, but it is the activation of a true creative ecosystem that acts both physically and on the social and economic development: many people from Favara and its environments got involved, young and old, creating job and volunteer opportunities for many in the community.

Based on the successful experience of FARM, a steady schedule of cultural activities of various entities has been programmed, although the group operates in extremely frugal conditions in terms of economic resources: urban gardens, shared green spaces and sensorial squares – as Zighizaghi – were created together with other places of art exhibition in the heart of the historical quarter. The economic sustainability is being implemented relying on specific activities of fundraising by numerous patrons, benefactors and supporters among individuals and private companies that share the spirit and the objectives of the project. Creative city and identity of places, experience economy and quality of life, cultural hubs and armatures, strategic planning and efficient good governance are not only new keywords to drive the urban development but integrated tools aimed at reactivating the urban organism re-encoding its cultural Dna, bringing practical resources and innovative procedures back in the game of the city development.

A CREATIVE URBAN AGENDA

Culture is more than the tangible part of sustainable development through the heritage or the intangible part through the creativity, but it's the "operative system" of the sustainable development: the collective intelligence that puts in connection tangible heritage and intangible identities, cultural infrastructures and creative economies, historical sites' conservation and urban innovation. As already mentioned this operative system for being powerful and context-oriented must be opensource, built by the several "coders" that act in the cultural ecosystem following a collective urban agenda for augmented cities and communities.

So, an effective creative urban agenda asks for practical actions, all grounded in local contexts and formulated and implemented through a collaborative approach, and a panel of initiatives that could act as the beta testers of the new creative-driven paradigm of sustainable development. We need five operative tools that could be implemented and tested for using culture and creativity as active tools in sustainable urban regeneration.

a) **Creative Labs:** integrated urban regeneration programs based on the development and consolidation of creative districts as living labs and incubators of ideas, culture, production and social development within which integrate and enhance public demand and decision-making, talents, resources' consumption reduction, energy efficiency and incentives with the opportunities for private entrepreneurship.

b) **Covenant of creativity:** drawing up of creative regeneration agreements or action plans formulated in highly participative ways in support of environmental and social sustainability, accompanied by monitoring benchmarks based on parameters related to the metabolism of buildings and public spaces, mobility, the waste cycle and the digital infrastructure. The value of culture and creativity for generating income and jobs has been largely proven. What should be measured first now is what is the cost of not valuing culture and creativity in urban planning.

c) **Creative capacity building:** activation of project-oriented, economic-driven and management-based local agencies or steering committees to enhance the creative cooperation at the city level contributing to foster the development of public-private-civil society partnerships and to attract investments, connected to a responsible simplification and to a greater effectiveness of the administration in the field of culture and creativity policies.

d) **Convergence and cross protocols:** developing positive convergences between the different creative sectors but also between them and the other sectors of the economy following integrated and transversal approaches and operative protocols based on exploration, co-creation, experimentation and evaluation. Creative urban policies have to encourage spill-overs and spin-offs and cross discipline collaboration.

e) **Creative dividend:** designing innovative tools for the creative city governance through the promotion of new culture-based frameworks for spreading the creativity's impact in everyday life. The creative dividend, through the six factors drawn in the external circle of the Diagram n.5 **(identity, dynamism, potentiality, multisectorality, interaction and development)**, acts on quality of life and spatial equalization, on environmental active protection, on people empowerment and social innovation, on multilevel governance and management incentives, on sustainable mobility, and on taxes and fiscal leverage. The structural interaction of six factors of creative dividend is able to enhance the social return on investment in culture and creativity and the spread of positive effects and effective impacts. The ethical dimension of culture and creativity needs a creativity dividend as an active instrument to improve the values' generation for reduce inequality and differences. We're moving from the creative economy to creativity in the economy as creativity is a catalyst leading to new business models in every sector, building notably in the opportunities offered by the alliance between digital technologies and social innovation.

The creative dividend must become an active part of the new rights to city and a money in the new marketplace of cultural capitalism. But, creativity on its own doesn't stand a chance for the cities. It's a contextual practice, one that needs spatial relations, efficient planning and responsible community. It asks for collaborative planning, sharing of ideas and active participation of the citizens. The creative dividend is the booster of the raising cultural welfare, because new perspectives are opening up for reshaping cultural policies with strategic and multidisciplinary alliances in favour of urban welfare. In the Augmented City the players in the cultural processes will have no option but to reorientate themselves towards a new alliance between institutional competences and social challenges. For the first time at the global level, the United Nations Sustainable Development Agenda for 2030 acknowledges the key role of culture, creativity and cultural diversity to solving sustainable development challenges. It highlighted the dual nature of cultural activities, goods and services: they have both an economic and a cultural dimension, providing jobs and revenues, driving innovation and sustainable economic growth, and at the same time conveying identities and values, fostering social inclusion and sense of belonging. We need to reshape cultural policies to redefine the role of culture and creativity in sustainable development (Unesco, 2015), but even more we must witness the multiple advantages of this fertile alliance, as a force for both social and economic sustainability, as a driver to promote human rights and fundamental freedoms.

So a creative-oriented urban agenda will bring about a positive transformation of the entire sphere of the arts, design, culture, a deep change in the mechanisms of price formation and distribution, a coming together of cultural communities, a development of more refined tastes and an improvement in the material situation of the creative class. The city augmented by creativity will make it possible to co-ordinate cultural initiatives targeted at territorially dispersed groups of consumers with demand, and will reshape the demand itself. It will help to enhance and spread cultural activities in order to make knowledge, cooperation, social innovation and to reactivate a productive metabolism.

CREATIVE CITY

01. Lyon Confluence (01.b) is one of the major urban project in Europe. The southern tip of Lyon's central peninsula, long devoted to manufacturing and transport, is the focus of an unprecedented project of urban renewal. Reclaimed from the waters in centuries past, this riverside site is re-embracing its banks and natural environment. The redevelopment is gradually highlighting an outstanding location and unique landscapes. Set to ultimately double the size of the city centre, this project is a rarity in Europe, a major challenge for the metropolitan area, and an opportunity for its residents. The dense quarter to the north, a residential park to the south called Le Champ, and various links (two bridges and a two-part footbridge) connect Lyon Confluence to the rest of the city. Phase Two's fundamentals are underpinned by the key notion of sustainable centrality. Phase Two of the Lyon Confluence urban project (in French: ZAC 2) was master-planned by the Herzog & de Meuron firm and landscapist Michel Desvigne. Some 30% of the existing market build-

01.a

ings will be conserved. Its balanced, mixed-use programme also aims to promote eco-friendly travel. This is why, in addition to the Market quarter and Le Champ, Phase Two features three new bridges: Pont Raymond Barre for the extended tramway; Pont des Girondins to connect Lyon Confluence and Gerland (on the Rhône's east bank); and La Transversale, a straight route for human-powered travel, including two footbridges over the Rhône and Saône. La Confluence is a lab for contemporary architecture. Besides being creative, the architecture must meet two essential criteria: quality of life and energy efficiency. This applies equally to housing, offices and public amenities. The **Cube Vert**, the HQ of television channel Euronews (01.a), is a reinterpretation of the curved roof of its neighbour, Les Salins du Midi, a former salt warehouse. But, most of all, its original way of creating patio atriums – truly wells of light – at each level. The building is designed by Jakob+MacFarlane. The **Musée des Confluences** by Coop Himmelb(l)au (01.c), understands itself not as an exclusive "Temple of the Muses" for the educated elite, but as a public gateway to the knowledge of our time. It stimulates a direct, active use—not only as a place of contemplation, but also as a meeting place in

the city. The striking interface situation of the construction site at the eponymous confluence of the Rhône and the Saône inspired the superposition in urban space of two complexly linked architectural units, crystal and cloud. The cloud structure, floating on pillars, contains a spatial sequence of black boxes— admitting no daylight, so as to achieve maximum flexibility for exhibition design.

By contrast, the crystal, rising towards the city side, functions as a transparent urban forum; it faces the city and receives visitors.

02. The Tetrarc agency has put its name to the **Hub Créatic** in Nantes, a building dedicated to young companies developing new digital applications. Behind its lively yellow walls, the building assembles seventy of these start-ups businesses. It has affirmed their presence in the town and offers them a scalable work space at a reduced rent where they can finalise their creations, live out the first moments of their existence and recognise their early development. The facility is characterized by its expressive yellow shading fins, which frame the windows with irregular trapezoidal forms. Each module takes a different geometry compared to its neighbors, creating a complex composition around the façades. The vibrant feature serves to create an identity for the structure, while also performing to reduce solar gain and thus creating more comfortable interiors. The layout is arranged around a central atrium distinguished by a dynamic screen of timber slats.

03. The **ONE Mile Project** is a multi-disciplinary collaborative effort to support the cultural production and socio-economic activity of Detroit's Oakland North End neighborhood. The project was conceived and designed by Akoaky (Anya Sirota and Jean Louis Farges) with the support of the Knight Arts Foundation, ArtPlace

America and Taubman College of Architecture and Urban Planning for activating events, exhibits, workshops, and performances. The first step of the project was in 2014 when the Mothership landed in an unmarked garage on Oakland Avenue and twelve members of Parliament-Funkadelic staged a special live performance. The Mothership is a P-Funk-inspired DJ booth, broadcast module, and urban marker for channeling the Afrofuturist sensibility of the legendary funk emblem. The unit activates an economically-challenged context, shifts perception, and creates value by transmitting vibrant, locally rooted performances and public events. By looking to local cultural production as a generative, enduring resource, the project reimagines design as an impactful social practice. The project is also an antidote to the broad renewal plan that erases important historical vestiges that connect Detroit and its cultural innovations to a greater national legacy.

04. Casa Netural in Matera (Italy), created in 2012, is a co-working rural and incubator of dreams, a neutral space of encounter and exchange. They have the goal of giving birth to business projects, innovative, generated by the meeting between local people and innovators from around the world. For the team of Casa Netural innovation has to be found outside of major urban centers, putting all the outlying regions and rural areas in terms of innovating. Casa Netural wants to be a landmark in the area and is proposed as the step missing between citizens bearers of dreams and the world of business incubators and startups, in an attempt to fill a gap that often relegates the dreams of everyone in a professional drawer. Casa Netural has not remained an isolated experiment but has generated many other creative colonies of creativity and social innovation that have become the cornerstone of the European Capital of Culture 2019. Today, Matera is a creative ecosystem in which many cultural epicenter interact and where creativity becomes a powerful catalyst for urban and human regeneration. The Open Design School, opened in 2016, is the first design school in Europe based on the principles of open culture that connects authors, bloggers, designers, artisans, hackers, students, professionals and academics. Matera and Basilicata use creativity to offer themselves as a European platform for radical innovation in the field of art, science and technology.

05. In 3rd Session of the Landscape Award of the Council of Europe 2012-2013 **Libera** initiative won a special mention for "Strengthening democracy". The project of the revival of Alto Belice Corleonese relates to the recovery of land from mafia organisations, which was illegally seized by them. This project of great interest encompasses a combination of the Council of Europe's principles: human rights, rule of law and democracy. Landscape is both the instrument and the result. The project is as much political as economic, and produces a landscape which highlights the local identity and culture. It restores the cultural dimension of the landscape and the quality of the natural environment. Organic production and local processing of farm products, the development of renewable energies and the restoration of the heritage all provide job opportunities for vulnerable populations. The outstanding level of volunteer mobilisation is one of the project's strong points.

06. FARM Cultural Park is a contemporary art complex that occupies the entire historic centre of Favara (Italy). The idea is to draw visitors in to a handful of structures entwined together like an art gallery — there's a design corner, a tea garden and a bookshop, a sandwich shop, a champagne bar, and a concept store. Exteriors of buildings are used as canvases for huge paintings and sculptures by artists such as Fabio Melosu; courtyards feature installations, including Fabio Novembre's giant pot-chairs; and one building houses the world's biggest permanent collection of work by US fashion photographer Terry Richardson. The idea came about when Bartoli bought several empty dwellings in Favara's semi-abandoned centre. Inspired by places such as Djemaa el-Fna in Marrakech, he thought that the maze of stone houses, with its alleys, central square and small castle were a perfect setting for an art marketplace, rather like a Sicilian kasbah. FARM is therefore a genuine workshop, a hothouse of social innovation. It's a space in which a community of locals and creative talents personally work on problems and intervention strategies, seeking to make the most of their resources, to reuse, regenerate, reinterpret, revitalise and cultivate. All the project is illuminated by the light of contemporary

art, of architecture and design, which lies at the centre of FARM's functional programme (a gallery, but also a place for artistic production, a residence for young artists, a workshop and educational facilities). But contemporary art also underpins an aesthetic enhancement of the ruins, which are displayed in a new way as part of a complex and stratified landscape, open to interpretation and transformation, and oriented to re-use and re-cycle, creatively enhancing the Re-cyclical Urbanism. The project is based on care and also has huge potential for a circular economy and a creative city. Indeed, having abandoned the idea that South Italy must grow to close the industrial gap with North Italy, this development model envisages an urban/human regeneration founded on the community engagement, on the values and identities of the local area, its interweaving of nature and history, and its abundance of flavours and traditions.

In 2017 FARM Cultural Park won the Curry Stone Design Prize, awarded each year to honour innovative projects that use design to address pressing social justice issues. The Prize acknowledges FARM's work in improving professional and public consciousness about the role of social design in urban regeneration.

07. The cooperative **Orto Capovolto** was born in Palermo (Italy) with the aim of contributing to the creation of a common vegetable garden at the city level, provincial, regional and national level through both awareness to environmental issues, agricultural and food that the establishment of Urban Farms (orchards and farms in urban and peri-urban) at different scales and with different orientations, in order to experience a better environmental, economic and social for cities and individuals who live there.

08. SOU. The School of Architecture for Children is the new ambitious project of Farm Cultural Park: educational activities after school, related to urban planning, architecture and the environment, community building, but also to art, design, urban agriculture and nutritional education will involve children, young people and their parents. The SOU's mission is to stimulate reflection, planning and action for the betterment of society. Promoting education in the host values, participation, tolerance and solidarity, generosity and social commitment. **Somewhere Someone is doing Something** was an educational/practice initiative led in 2015 by Urbanism Chair of the University of Palermo aimed to experiment some tactical urbanism actions for reimagining Favara starting by the FARM. The urban design project realized several pop-up urbanism actions spread along the seven courtyards in order to redefine spaces, functions and uses as a node of a wide network that connect Favara to Palermo and to the world. The project was realized by the students of the Urban Design Studio as an interactive exhibition where professional skills and people dreams could redefine together public spaces, pedestrian path, waste recycle protocols, community garden management, sharing welfare, etc.

In Re-cyclical Urbanism the scrap resources, the residues of development and functional disposals can contribute in a more creative and less erosive way to reshape the manner in which we move, to close the energy cycles, to re-weave creative relationships with the environment to produce new landscape and to feed cultures settlement not only capable of activating new urban metabolism, but also to react proactively to decline scenarios.

6. RE-CYCLICAL

THE RE-CYCLICAL URBANISM

A paradigm shift for the circular metamorphosis

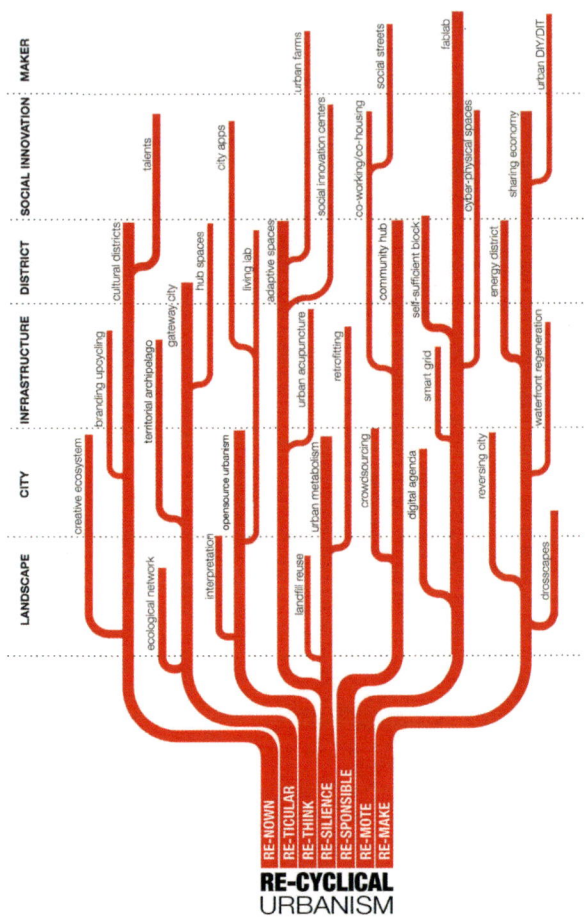

RE-IMAGINING URBANISM IN THE CIRCULAR SOCIETY

When Eugene Stoermer introduced the term "Anthropocene" to denote the consequences to the planet of the industrial revolution due to humankind's acceleration of territorial, structural and climate changes1, he could not have imagined that, over the last twenty years, a pervasive "anthropo-development" would have produced such anabolic effects as to make the human footprint on the planet so enormous. This footprint has been mistaken for that of a deity — a seductive demon — and has been the object of a permeating idolatry of endless growth. The aporias of this worship have given us comfort, leading to a steady erosion of territorial resources — land being the most evident and alarming synecdoche. Together with the land, the identity structures of the cultural palimpsests and the vegetation patterns of cities have been depleted; vital metabolisms have been anesthetized, water and waste cycles disrupted and mobility cycles have become inflexible, making them useless. The ability of urban settlements to maintain the necessary relations with their rural components has worn away. The productive and generative capacity of local factories has been suppressed by anesthetizing endogenous development factors. The regenerative value of maintaining buildings and of caring for places has been forgotten and natural circular territorial processes have been cut off or rerouted.

In the US the expansive model has produced suburban sprawl and the dramatic polarization between metropolis and rural towns with the result of urban desertification in the wider range of the Rust Belt of industrial decline and the dramatic decline of cities like Detroit, Philadelphia, Cleveland and Baltimore (Ryan, 2014).

In Europe, the model produced a settlement system characterized by a steady erosion of urban resources, land being the most evident and alarming synecdoche. Since the mid-fifties to the present the total area of urban areas increased by 78% while the population growth was just 33%, with an acceleration of 9% between 1990 and 2006. To contrast the erosive model and dissipative, for nearly a decade, the European Commission is committed to encouraging more sustainable land use (EC-Regional Policy, 2011), by implementing concrete actions to mitigate the negative effects of waterproofing and to wake osmotic cycles of water and vegetation, new blue and green infrastructures for development. But in 2010 the overall objective of the revision of the development has become, thanks to the impulse of the European Climate Foundation, a clear roadmap towards resource-efficient Europe, which aims to reach zero net land degradation by 2050 (ECF, 2010).

We need to play a leading role in a structural change in which cities — in their metropolitan, reticular and rur-urban forms — are called upon to reactivate their territorial wealth, guided by urban planning that is able to guarantee new ways of converging cultural, economic, environmental and social sustainability. Not just by adopting renewed visions of the future or using new paradigms, but above all, by means of effective decisions, quality projects, and efficient processes. More advanced urban planning, which is more sensitive to identities and more geared towards innovation, is prompted to take on the responsibility of renewing the conditions of its existence, role, and involvement. As well as to reconsider its own epistemological core in relation to new sources and forms of knowledge and to consequently review its toolbox, replacing some worn-out regulatory instruments with more effective planning tools capable of acting jointly with the increasing number of non-institutional urban planning practices.

I believe that we are witnessing the birth of the first forms of a **Re-cyclical Urbanism**, based on the recycling of areas, infrastructure, and landscapes and driven by adaptive and incremental circular processes. It is essential to investigate evidence of these processes and practices already underway to identify their parentage, recognize their epistemology, define protocols, but above all, shape the design devices needed to reimagine urbanism in the era of circular transition (Carta, 2016).

The European Commission has clearly stated that a more intelligent, sustainable and competitive development requires a paradigm shift in which the territory is construed as a primary resource, considered the holder of "development cells", which are too often underused or mystified with regard to their real potential for use (EC, Directorate-General for Research and Innovation, 2012).

Cities designed and built on land rent — on which Italy set a benchmark — need to be replaced with cities of social and cultural profitability, value creation and jobs production. Cities that recycle already-used land to avoid energy waste, smarter cities — not just technologically, but also wiser and more sentient ones, capable of activating collective intelligence —, and cities that are more dialogic and shared, and therefore more responsible.

The European strategy contained in Horizon 2020 clearly states the need to use the potential of "urban mines" (dismissed landfills, abandoned areas, infrastructure and buildings), adapting new urban policies to the lifecycle approach (Life Cycle Assessment): from the procurement of raw materials (vacant land and abandoned buildings) to the end of the cycle (new uses and functions), using as little energy and resources as possible and, instead, reactivating latent energy.
The issue is not only the reuse of materials, spaces, buildings or urban scrap, but rather the need to define a paradigm of the renewal of the cycles, that is, the re-cycle as regeneration - architectural, cultural, social and economic - of urban settlements through placing into new life cycles of urban complexes, settlement tissues and infrastructure networks under disposal, changing or reduced function. Re-cycling cities, to experience growth without expansion and development without consumption, it means not only to use the ruins / materials of urban mines in development metamorphosis, it means acting on the innovation of styles / life cycles, on behaviors / values and especially on regulation / design of the re-settlement.
In Re-cyclical Urbanism the scrap resources, the residues of development and functional disposals can contribute in a more creative and less erosive way to reshape the manner in which we move, to close the energy cycles, to re-weave creative relationships with the environment

to produce new landscape and to feed cultures settlement not only capable of activating new urban metabolism, but also to react proactively to decline scenarios.

CITIES IN THE CIRCULAR ECONOMY

Cities will have to act within a new evolutionary model, the result of innovation produced by the third industrial revolution and by start-ups, the actions of makers, and energy generated by creativity and by the metamorphosis of the circular economy. An urban model that is more responsible and capable of reshaping the objectives of tangible and intangible asset production, of revising energy and mobility protocols, and above all, of rethinking the settlement model: a new holistic way of thinking that elicits reuse, recycling and creative evolution within next-generation capitalism — "Capitalism 4.0", about which Kaletsky (2010) writes — which generates an economy — the Next Economy proposed and elaborated by Brugmans, van Dinteren and Hater (2016) — created from the integration of renewable energies and circular economy, able to produce new value from the re-cyclical processes of the new urban metabolism. The task of administrators, urban planners, architects, citizens, and enterprises is to work on urban settlements characterized by cycle flows — some still vital, others produced by surplus and by the overproduction of changing urban complexes. It is also to work on the rhythms of the discontinued urban fabric and transforming infrastructure networks, which need to be addressed through their modification, removal or reinvention, thanks to which the components are recreated, without destroying them, by changing their functions in pursuit of a generative view and increasing their creative resilience.

Recycling is not only one of the main keywords of the design action of urban planning, architecture and design (Ciorra, Marini, 2011; Fabian, Munarin, 2017), but is also one of the most powerful guiding thoughts in the transformation from a wasteful linear economy to a regenerative circular one for cities and territories that wish to pursue sustainability, quality and creativity (Carta, Ronsivalle, 2015). In a circular economy, there are two types of material flows: organic ones, capable of being replenished in the biosphere, and technical ones, destined to increase in value in a system in which all activities, starting from mining and manufacturing, are organized so that the waste of one phase becomes a resource for the following phase. According to the principles of the circular economy, nothing is waste and everything that is discarded from one production process is the raw material for another production process. Moreover, the very design of a product is based on the possibility of dismantling its parts and reusing them in subsequent production cycles, based on supply chain cooperation and new production networks: a more creative "planned recycling" instead of consumerist planned obsolescence. The Circular Growth paradigm aims to change the current linear system on which our industrial society is based into a cyclical system, replacing the process "produce, use and discard" with a more fertile "produce, use and reuse" (Ellen MacArthur Foundation, 2012).

A circular society demands new political responsibility — and responsibility for urban planning — so that cities may once again be welcoming to people, attractive of ideas, generative for businesses, and supportive to the community archipelagos. It requires the implementation of concrete actions to guarantee a new balance between rural, urban and developable, between landscaping weft and infrastructural warp, not just placing limits on the indiscriminate use of land, but above all, stimulating, encouraging and rewarding the reuse of already urbanized areas and the densification of functions.

Planning cities in the era of the Neo-Anthropocene and of the circular metabolism means rejecting the consolation of a molecular approach and accepting the challenge of an organic ecosystem approach, allowing ourselves to be guided by a new long-sighted vision to look towards the innovation horizon, but also to look back and retrieve wisdom, rituals and structurally self-sufficient circular practices not yet seduced by the demon of anthropic development. We also need effective paradigms and concrete projects, or commitments, to serve a discipline of urban planning that knows how to influence the urban metabolism, recombining the genetic code contained in the areas and flows to be put back into circulation. Although often fragmented or weakened, these flows are still able to generate new fabric if reactivated by the vital energy produced by the cycles of water, food, energy, nature, waste, people and goods. Flows which have an impact on the daily life of cities and which inevitably act on a large scale, contributing to the reticular connection of settlements. Reconnecting them with a holistic view of the metabolism is one of the greatest challenges to urban planners, designers, administrators and citizens who aim to give new impetus to the circular Neo-Anthropocene, connecting its technical components with its social and moral dimensions (Sijmons, 2014). Not enough then enter the sensitivity to recycling in traditional urban and regional planning processes, but need a disruptive innovation paradigms, decision processes and planning instruments: need a real Re-cyclical Urbanism.

Re-cyclical Urbanism, therefore, not only works on the tangible potential (areas, volumetric dimensions, infrastructure, landscapes), but also on the potential related to the memories and identities contained in the areas to be put back into circulation. It is from these areas that 21st-century cities will have to produce new urban intelligence, firstly by rewriting abandoned "lines of code" (functions), reactivating unused "memory banks" (areas), and reclaiming inefficient urban "routines" (infrastructure). These are all urban materials still containing traces of vitality, which in many practices today provide resources for ecological planning and urban agriculture, infrastructure for sustainable mobility and self-sufficient production, crowdsourcing tasks, and places for sharing and social innovation.

Making the city re-cyclical thus means abandoning the traditional erosive linear logic to adopt a new "development operating system" — no longer closed and preset, but open source — which is not only enriched by the contribution of the various users but learns from experiences, adapting to spatial, social and economic contexts instead of stiffening them within predefined standards and rules. An operating system — urban planning intelligence — capable of generating a more sustainable, more responsible and also more creative city, and capable of rethinking urban community models to reinvent settlement forms, firstly by reactivating urban assets that have fallen into disuse, are undergoing change, or are in crisis. An intelligent city capable of reshaping the way we move, weaving new creative relationships with the environment and the landscape, and fuelling the production of urban settlement cultures, which can reactivate the vital organs of the city and its life cycles, but also react to deterioration scenarios. Cities of the future, particularly medium-sized Mediterranean cities — the true antidote to the world's megalopolises — must act within a new capitalism that no longer works as a linear set of financial instructions, but as an evolutionary circular system that reinvents itself and is strengthened by crisis — that learns from crisis — and is able to provide a guide to settlement processes through strong integration with ecological sustainability, regional planning, land-use management, energy efficiency, and morphology planning without withdrawing from the production of value. The new urban operating system will leave behind the linear code of the obsolete 3Rs (resources, revenue, regulation) to adopt the circular code of the new 3Rs: recycling, resilience, and reactivation. However, in order for them not to remain an ineffectual mantra and to be capable of generating new planning practices and urban devices, the new three keywords must be integrated into a renewed "urban ecosystem".

SEVEN PARADIGMS OF THE RE-CYCLICAL URBANISM

For those, like myself, who take a militant approach to seeking a new urban ecosystem, there is now much empirical evidence showing the presence of re-cyclical urbanism, and to sort through it, I have developed a concept map as a flow diagram representing the ramifications and evidence of each of the seven main paradigmatic branches: identity, polycentrism, knowledge, resilience, democracy, sharing, and regeneration (**Diagram n. 6**). To specify the traces, latent evidences and experimentations underway for each of the paradigms, I have defined how, with what concrete actions, and by means of which projects the recycling challenge intercept with the various levels of the landscape and peri-urban areas (landscape), the city and the urban systems (city), infrastructure and networks (infrastructure), neighborhoods, buildings and public spaces (districts), social innovation (social innovation), and digital craftsmen (makers), identifying ramifications, origins and offspring in order to trace a map that can give us our bearings and guide subsequent experimentation.

Using the "RE-" prefix, which characterizes the re-cyclical approach, I've called the first branch **RE-NOWN** because it represents the paradigm of identity as urban reputation, which is essential in facilitating greater identification by inhabitants and users with the new circular metabolism. The first level on which it acts is the city, which, through creative ecosystems, is once again an educational factor in the community and an opportunity for knowledge and training (Marseille, Euroméditerranée). At the infrastructure level, we witness the branded upcycling of viaducts or abandoned railways which are enriched by urban marketing actions to strengthen their regenerative effort (Lowline Park in New York; the IM Viadukt in Zurich; the Atlanta Beltline). At the level of architecture and public space, cultural districts are increasingly re-elaborating new forms, places and relations that contain and connect the flows of information and communication the city generates with increasing frequency, scale and speed, especially starting from its latent cultural resources (Farm Cultural Park, Favara). Finally, social innovation is implemented and accelerated by the role of talents in reactivating cities, both in the redevelopment of spaces and in the notoriety and reputation of cities (Mapa del Talent, Barcelona; Mappa dei Talenti, Palermo). The second branch is **RE-TICULAR** and supports the paradigm of polycentrism, striving to create new social aggregation hubs that fluidize settlements, occupying places undergoing change and reusing them for social occasions as new activators. It acts firstly on the landscape, restoring ecological networks in a planning perspective that redefines functions and ways of using the natural and anthropic components, restoring the grid of agricultural production that has given structure to the European landscape throughout the centuries, reclaiming old railway routes, re-naturalizing infrastructure that has fallen into disuse and reactivating agricultural functions (Natuurbrug Zanderij Crailo Ecoduct, Netherlands). At the city and infrastructure level, territorial archipelagos accelerate the affirmation of new supra-local values that allow new semantic cycles to be activated in areas of undergoing transformation and discontinued areas of cities transitioning from local egoism to a reticular and polycentric dimension (Randstadt Holland; Poland Reticular Strategy). Specifically, gateway cities of the global system belong to the infrastructure level and serve as hubs in the reactivation of local cycles by tapping into the energy produced by global flows (Amsterdam, Rotterdam, Barcelona). The consequence at the district level is the proliferation of hub spaces that facilitate the localization of urban places structured into archipelagos of competitive clusters in the various fields of development. Their task is to help new service-sector or urban manufacturing businesses revitalize the urban hubs by favouring their localization in recycled areas at a lower settlement cost (Impact Hub Global Network; Nantes, Hub Creatic).

RE-THINK is the paradigm of new forms of knowledge, which are able to act on urban communication by planning opportunities and designing places in which knowledge of the urban system arises from specialisms and becomes widespread knowledge, intersubjective competence and new collective thinking, becoming concrete material for an agreement for the co-existence of urban populations and the resulting development pact. Belonging to this paradigm are the now consolidated US and French experiences of interpretation, which have generated a spread of plans for the interpretation of natural and cultural landscapes to guide the use of the cultural armature, reactivating the cycles of knowledge, education and sustainable tourism (Site Unesco du Pont du Garde nella Région Languedoc-Roussillon). At the city level, sustainable development policies are defining and consolidating veritable open source urbanism that systematizes the widespread knowledge constantly produced by the population and by local stakeholders to produce a new integrated system of sensors and actuators that makes urban policies more effective and less dissipative (Office for Civic Innovation in San Francisco). Living labs are a product at the district level that increasingly enliven towns by providing places to encourage open and shared innovation, complementing technical knowledge, innovative processes and social demand with a public-private partnership (Sant Cugat LOW3 in Barcelona; the Centquatre in Paris). Social innovation is incited by the continuous creation of city apps for smartphones and mobile and wearable devices that are revolutionizing the relationship between questions and answers, sensors and actuators, active citizenship and proactive administrations (Renurban; Boskoi for mapping edible landscapes; Twitter Mapping by Fischer).

The **RE-SILIENCE** branch channels the lifeblood of resilience and environmental sustainability and encourages us to adopt a flexible and dialogue-based attitude in which the flexibility of functions, the permeability of spaces and the adaptability of settlements are no longer addressed as purely conceptual and spatial problems, but are examined in relation to the social, economic and technological result which today becomes part of building a city, becoming issues/instruments/regulations for planning urban resilience. New peri-urban landscapes created by recycling garbage dumps are becoming more frequent as new vital systems capable of producing places of leisure and generators of power from the waste cycle (Freshkills Park, New York). The resilience paradigm produces practices and creates neighborhoods or entire cities with a new urban metabolism, which are capable of better handling climate change or hydrogeological changes and of absorbing floods, producing new fluid urban forms especially from public spaces. Water, for example, even flood water, becomes project material to be absorbed by parks, roads and permeable squares, both to alleviate the sewage system, and to create new collective spaces in connection with water, giving them breath (Rotterdam Urban Metabolism; Saint-Kjelds Climate Adaptation

District, Copenhagen; BIG U project, New York). The infrastructure level is the subject of specific resilience activities with the retrofitting of roads, railway areas, sewage systems and waterways to make them more suited to energy efficiency requirements and to the challenges of climate change. Belonging to the same level are urban acupuncture experiments aimed at reactivating the life cycles of deteriorating or stagnated neighborhoods. The reactivation of urban capital can occur by leveraging small pressure points in the city, giving rise to a positive repercussion affecting large areas, covering the functional, infrastructural, cultural and social networks of the cities (Curitiba: acupuncture strategies applied to the city were used as the best solution to solve the critical issues of the contemporary city and enabled it to win the Globe Sustainable City Award in 2010). New adaptive urban spaces are the increasingly frequent outcome of the evolution of tactical urbanism, in which the reactivation of the urban resources on a micro-scale and by micro-players is favored over large-scale programs requiring the use of large amounts of capital. The new spaces that readapt abandoned areas and buildings in a transitioning city also contribute to providing responses to a compelling demand for social resilience, leading to the creation of veritable social innovation centers in districts and communities. These encourage the sharing of spaces and skills to ease empowerment with regard to the new challenges of the future (Centre for Social Innovation in New York), as well as the rise of actual urban farms that bring agriculture back to the city beyond the rhetoric of urban horticolture, making them a powerful engine of new social relations and a power supply for renewed urban economies (Sociopolis, Valencia; Agropolis, Munich; Greening Detroit; Hackney City Farm).

The paradigm of participatory democracy upholds the **RE-SPONSIBLE** branch, which requires communication to nourish improvement of the collaborative dimension and efficiency of the plans themselves, fostering widespread environments of awareness/action more suited to contemporary social and environmental needs. The first effect is the extension of crowdsourcing to urban policies, by means of a new proactive use of citizenship as a permanent system of sensors/actuators. New argumentative ethics of planning must become a vehicle for interpersonal relations, a creator of responsibility and activator of the mobilization of collective intelligence surrounding the urban project through the spread of community hub networks. Less and less are these physical and institutional places, but rather, increasingly open and shared, creating social innovation around themselves by means of an increasingly widespread system of co-working and co-housing that overcomes the initial logic of the need to share costs to participate in a powerful ethics and aesthetics of sharing urban space (The Embassy Network: shared housing for people with digital and creative talent). Within this paradigm, makers are steadily emerging from their digital laboratories, and citizens from their associations, to produce social streets, with the goal of making their sensitivity, skills and professionalism available to the local community. They can, therefore, establish a bond, share necessities and exchange knowledge in order to carry out collective projects of common interest and thus reap all the benefits arising from greater social interaction (Via Fondazza in Bologna and over 300 of its followers).

RE-MOTE is the sharing paradigm that has produced the open source city in which we live, which requires a high level of synergy between the new poly-centrality of services, the molecular building structure required by new forms of living, and the constant supply of increasingly wireless and cloud-based governance as application of the digital agenda. The new urban fabrics arising from reuse are increasingly imbued with digital components (sensors, apps, social networking, civic dashboards) that are made and remade between producer and consumer, intercepting the demands of increasingly prosumer citizens (Ratti, Claudel, 2016). The digital cycle connects the perceptions and requirements of functionality and comfort of inhabitants, complementing them with their requests for knowledge and experience and with the demand for democracy and supply of cooperation (Smart Citizen Initiative for the shared monitoring of environmental quality; Place Pulse, an experiment of open source mapping of urban perception). At the infrastructure and district level, the increasingly consolidated and effective testing of smart grids for intelligent energy management is changing the traditional model of delocalized energy production with inefficient and costly distribution in favor of a model that not only brings production closer to consumption but also sustainably synchronizes supply and demand. Experiments regarding energetically self-sufficient blocks are of great interest. They reshape the settlement space using a multi-purpose solution that involves the interaction of the residential space, the production space related to new urban factories, and the space related to the return of urban agriculture, connected by new collection and self-recycling of waste, with the self-production of photovoltaic, micro wind power or even power from the photosynthesis of algae (Solarschiff in Freiburg; the Bed Zed Pavilion in London; the Algae-Powered Building in Hamburg). All this contributes to deep social innovation, produced by the union between the digital and physical space, creating the conditions to reactivate the new collective city by means of new forms and ways of using public space. Fab labs and digital craftsmen increasingly take the new leading role in the contemporary city that once again becomes a productive and manufacturing city (KPMG, 2016). They present themselves as an archipelago of micro-players in the economy – but also in politics and society – in the third industrial revolution, contributing to the return of manufacturing in abandoned warehouses, reactivating craftsmanship and establishing cooperative networks with research and industry, often forming actual makers quarters. Today there are over 350 fab labs throughout the world and Italy has the third highest number of them, following the United States and France (the Fab Lab at MIT in Cambridge, the Fab City project in Barcelona and the new Manifattura in Rovereto give us three different interpretations of the urban role of makers). Finally, **RE-MAKE** is the branch concerning the regeneration of public space. It not only activates places of social interaction, but also provides incentives for the rebirth of new professions and revived urban factories alongside the traditional ones that have survived extensive industrialization, revitalizing them, adjusting ancient artisan knowledge and adapting it to the changed demands of new and more aware consumers. The city of innovative professions and the productive city of the manufacturing renaissance will require, more and more often, not only the use of creativity, strategic vision, economic and fiscal support, and innovative management, but also integrated projects and urban planning tactics for the collective space, accompanied by a constant assessment of the effects of choices and performance monitoring. The new creative and innovative ecosystem of cities more and more often arises firstly from new public spaces, from landscapes of agricultural transformation, and from parasitic structures that colonize abandoned, idle or underused urban areas with increasing frequency, producing new and more attractive urban lattices that can be accessed in multiple ways and which connect the new cultural, educational, and ecological functions to production. These are drosscapes, formed from the scraps produced by the evolution of cities, considered interstitial, in-between spaces in the urban fabric, free strips along the roads, archipelagos of parking lots, unused land, areas waiting for development, waste dumping sites, cargo storage districts: an endless and pervasive stretch of breaks and perimeters that frame the residential neighborhoods. They are areas that accumulate in the process of post-Fordist deindustrialization and technological innovation and which can once again accommodate the new urban factories. They are sites of the reversing city, made up of places of transition and less and less residual spaces, and increasingly the new protagonists in the re-cycle oriented project. Infrastructure subject to review and recycling increasingly includes those of ports and peri-portal areas — urban waterfronts as activators of fluid cities (Ronsivalle, 2016), as urban regenerators through the energy of flows crossing them (an example is Hafencity in Hamburg). Playing a leading role in the regeneration paradigm are the new energy districts, capable of integrating and promoting public demand, reduced consumption, energy and fiscal incentives, and private requirements for redevelopment projects. Their feasibility will have to be substantiated by drawing up energy agreements in support of the districts, in the face of environmental sustainability and social projects, assessed on recycling parameters regarding the buildings, public spaces, mobility, the waste cycle and digital infrastructure (the EcoQuartier de Bonne in Grenoble or the Eco-quartiers Flaubert et Luciline in Rouen). Social innovation is encouraged through the pervasiveness of the sharing economy, which is reaching significant results and dimensions, whether it be the sharing of goods, services, information, spaces, time or skills, bartering between individuals or companies, crowding, or making, that is, self-production from hobbies to digital fabrication, radically transforming the fields of tourism (Airbnb), transport (car and bike sharing; Uber), energy, food (Food sharing initiatives) and design. Urban making is also being strongly driven by DIY (Do It Yourself) and DIT (Do It Together) urban practices by means of which groups of citizens, residents, temporary users, travellers, urban hackers and urban farmers reactivate places, manage abandoned sites, take care of public spaces, and maintain or co-manage collective services (tactical urbanism; pop-up city).

TOWARDS A REVERSE URBANISM

Concluding this first conceptual description - that will require further study, field testing and review - we can say that the Re-cyclical Urbanism, not content to be an effective keyword or a powerful totem, but called planners, decision-makers and local actors to the commitment of a new responsibility and a new hermeneutics of plan and project that is not satisfied with a fruitful disruptive innovation but ask for a generative creativity. It requires attention to places, sharing of knowledge, care of identities, relationships and reactivation of productions that return to power life cycles, to cultivate talents of the people, to strengthen the social ecosystem, to attract ideas, to generate innovation, to produce new economies and to strengthen solidarity networks. Before the emergence of many informal practices and tactics, before the explosion of urban social innovation, we must have the courage to implement a true **reverse urbanism**, an extraction process of knowledge, design and planning from urban resources for their re-use, reactivation and recycling according to information produced by an abductive process that reconstructs strategies, standards, rules and design starting from the practices, from ongoing experiments, and from the experience of success, even when partial. The process of reverse urbanism not only applies to positive solutions, but also requires disassembly and study of urban and rural junkspaces, water cycles, brownfields and derelict infrastructures, in order to understand their generative wealth, analyzing their components still active, in order to extract new paradigms or lost wisdoms. The action of a recycling urbanism is not limited to reconstruct methods or processes, but should be especially geared to extract new forms of action capable of acting on urban and regional resources not previously considered or underestimated. The rediscovery of the richness of "inverse city", according to Bernardo Secchi, which has the voids as central elements, and that is structured starting from the intermediate waiting spaces, the great outdoors and the natural scenery, should match a reverse urbanism who can act with new cognitive protocols, appropriate design devices and innovative spatial and social configurations: new "social rhythms" open, dialogic and circular must come from residues of previous "idiorrhythmes", *à la Barthes*, closed, separated and linear.

FROM UP-CYCLE TO HYPER-CYCLE

01. A **Circular Economy** seeks to rebuild capital, whether this is financial, manufactured, human, social or natural. This ensures enhanced flows of goods and services. The system diagram, developed by Ellen MacArthur Foundation, illustrates the continuous flow of technical and biological materials through the "value circle". The more we can make our economy circular, the more sustainable it will become in ecological terms. This idea is also opposed to our current economic model, in which raw materials are turned into products which are destroyed after use. The basic principle of the linear model is that used products no longer have economic usefulness and that their remains can be returned to nature without problems or costs. Not only after use, but also during production. In **Vitoria-Gasteiz** (Spain), 2012 European Green Capital, the belt of suburbs has been the subject of an ambitious project for the conversion of spaces and uses, to be reconnected with the city centre, redefining their scope and identity through a **Green Belt** spreading over more than 800 Ha.

02. Ecoduct along Highway A50 (Netherlands): this wildlife bridge provides a safe crossing path for wildlife amidst the danger of highways. Several European countries have been using various crossing structures to reduce the conflict between wildlife and roads for several decades and use a variety of overpasses and underpasses to protect and reestablish wildlife cycles.

03. Considering landscape Project by the Oslo School of Architecture and Design. The projected started with the revelation of the scenic landscape at Gjersrud Stensrud. The area contains a long-stretching stream connected with fluctuating green structure; it contains bigger lakes used for recreational purpose, old forest, old farms and their fields, and it is located next to "Østmarka". In the environment of this green structure the site holds a valuable biodiversity, with even threatened plants, insects, animals and birds. As a paradox Gjersrud Stensrud has been planned for development several times, as it is Oslo's last and big undeveloped area. Urbanization is going to change the biodiversity in the area. The project works with this relationship. As a start we looked at which areas could be used for building when setting the nature first. As of today Norway has less than 2 % forest protection, but as planners we can make decisions which are critical for these nature types and the creatures living there. By incorporating the biodiversity and its assumed changes in the urbanization process the project's wish was to make a good functioning area, planned for a long time perspective.

04. At 2,200 acres, **Freshkills Park** will be almost three times the size of Central Park and the largest park developed in New York City in over 100 years. The transformation of what was formerly the world's largest landfill into a productive and beautiful cultural destination will make the park a symbol of renewal and an expression of how our society can restore balance to its landscape. In addition to providing a wide range of recreational opportunities, including many uncommon in the city, the park's design, ecological restoration and cultural and educational programming will emphasize environmental sustainability and a renewed public concern for our human impact on the earth. Freshkills Park will host an incredible variety of public spaces and facilities for social, cultural and physical activity, for learning and play. The site is large enough to support many sports and programs that are unusual in the city, including horseback riding, mountain biking, nature trails, kayaking, and large scale public art.

05. The **Lowline** is a plan to use innovative solar technology to illuminate a historic trolley terminal on the Lower East Side of New York City. The vision is a stunning underground park, providing a beautiful respite and a cultural attraction in one of the world's most dense, exciting urban environments. The proposed location is the one-acre former Williamsburg Bridge Trolley Terminal, just below Delancey Street on the Lower East Side of Manhattan. The site was opened in 1908 for trolley passengers, but has been unused since 1948 when trolley service was discontinued. Despite six decades of neglect, the space still retains some incredible features, like remnant cobblestones, crisscrossing rail tracks and vaulted ceilings. It is also directly adjacent to the existing JMZ subway track at the

Essex Street subway stop— so park visitors and subway riders would interact daily. This hidden historic site is located in one of the least green areas of New York City— presenting a unique opportunity to reclaim unused space for public good.

06. Matadero Music Academy (Madrid) is an up-cycle example. The use of this unit of the former slaughterhouse as a music production centre required three recording studios to be built. The construction containing these stands on a concrete slab and the acoustic insulation is dealt with using huge exterior enclosure elements. On the outside, the vertical walls have been built using sandbags mostly covered over with a green wall. On the inside, the walls comprise a corrugated sheet envelope, an internal layer of rock wool panels and a final plasterboard. All the unused materials of the dismissed site was up-cycled for activating the recyclical metabolism of the cultural centre.

07. Letten Viaducts (Zurich). In the summer of 2004, the project submitted by EM2N architects and their partner Zulauf Seippel Schweingruber Landscape Architects were chosen as the winners of the architectural competition for the redevelopment of the viaduct arches and the design of the Lettenviaduktweg. IM VIADUKT was planned as a meeting place for citizens of the district and its visitors. In 2011, the viaduct constructions were awarded three architectural prizes. At street level this railway viaduct was a barrier, full of derelict sheds and warehouses. The new retail front – a sub-cycle approach – has the area buzzing with activity and ensures the permeability of the infrastructure with frequent wide and safe access points to the pedestrian viaduct and pedestrian walkways between the neighbourhoods it used to separate. Using new materials in the interior space has been restricted with the aim to safeguard the potential of the arches. Tenants of the premises can choose from several options for interior layouts proposed by the architects.

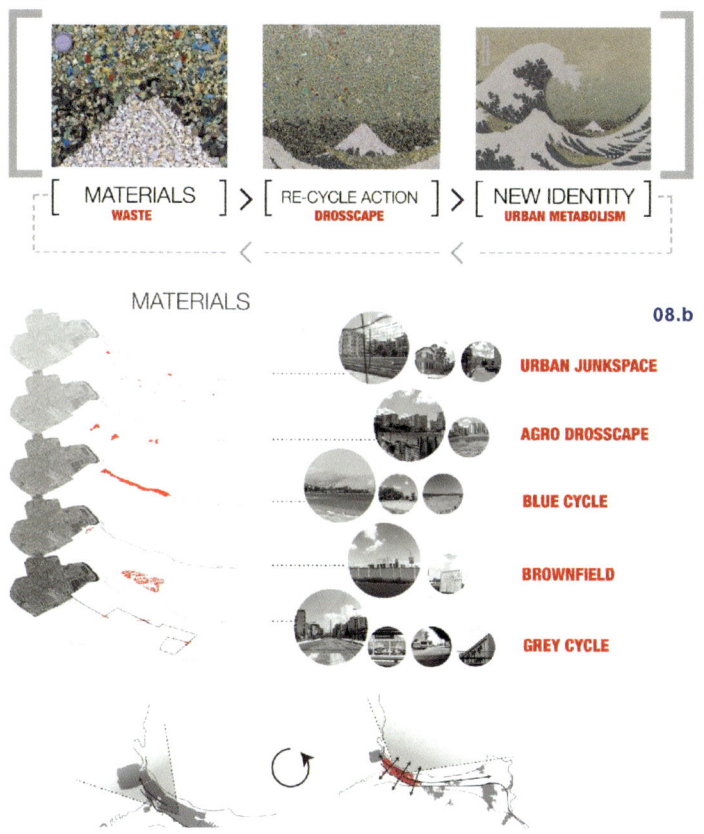

08.a MATERIALS (WASTE) > RE-CYCLE ACTION (DROSSCAPE) > NEW IDENTITY (URBAN METABOLISM)

08.b MATERIALS: URBAN JUNKSPACE, AGRO DROSSCAPE, BLUE CYCLE, BROWNFIELD, GREY CYCLE

08. PMO/re-verse "Hyper-cycling Palermo South Waterfront". The workshop was part of the Re-cycle Italy project, aimed to develop a "reverse urbanism" a process of extracting knowledge, design and planning information from urban resources to re-use and re-activating or recycling them based on the extracted information. The reverse urbanism process involves disassembling something (urban and rural junkspaces, dismissed blue, brown and grey cycles) and analyzing its active components and workings in detail. The

PMO
:Re-VERSE

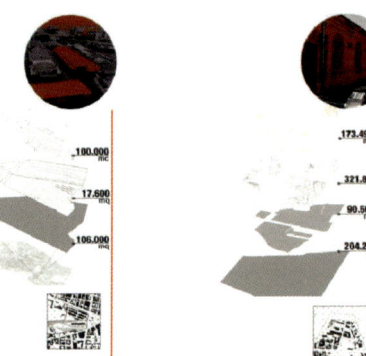

RE-CYCLE
ITALY

Workshop PMO/re-verse is a collective challenge to start from the reverse geography of the city, to reactivate the many cycles interrupted, latent, implicit or forgotten that characterize the South Coast of Palermo. Reverse look was used to generate a new vision of the future of the metropolitan city, but also a reverse urbanism may allow the evolutionary leap to a urban organism not only more resilient, but profitably more resistant to the metamorphosis of the development that the crisis requires us. PMO/re-verse is a reflection in action, an aggregate of sensors and a magma of actuators: planners, decision makers, managers, active citizens and makers have produced a powerful collective intelligence that gave new impulse to the variegated raw material to turn it into a new urban metabolism. For the Palermo South Coast is not enough of a wake cycles, but requires strategic action of Hyper-Cycling, a succession of restarts of life cycles that gradually reactivate all resources, both materials that those assets, creating a powerful "urban bootstrapping" able to start a process self-sustainable recursive.

In the Urban Age the world population is growing at a considerable rate. How long nature will be able to keep us with this is the main challenge for us. Climate change, water scarcity and rising resource prices show at an increasing rate that nature's abilities are not inexhaustible. A resilience-oriented city, therefore, must have insight into its own metabolism. When we look at, plan and manage cities as organisms with their own metabolisms it becomes clear that they are not separate entities.

# 7. RESILIENT

THE PROACTIVE ECOLOGY
Resilient, circular and self-sufficient cities

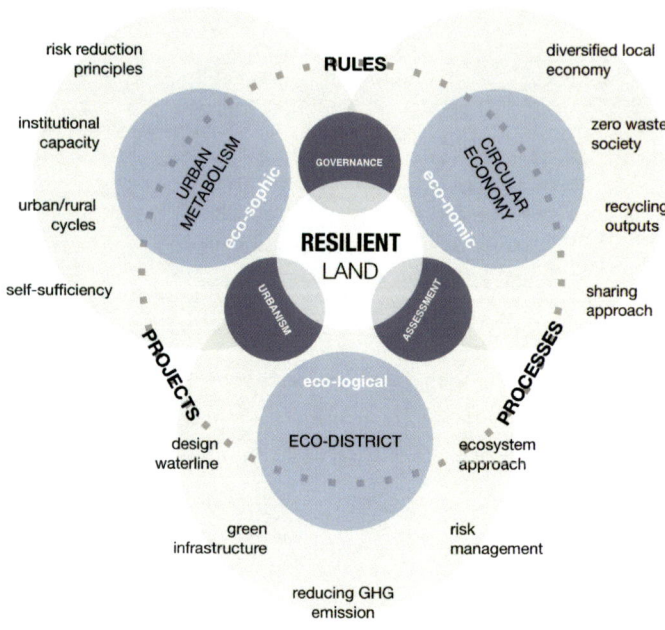

THE RESILIENCE REVOLUTION

In the Urban Age the world population is growing at a considerable rate. How long nature will be able to keep us with this is the main challenge for us. Climate change, water scarcity and rising resource prices show at an increasing rate that nature's abilities are not inexhaustible. A resilience-oriented city, therefore, must have insight into its own metabolism. When we look at planning and managing cities as organisms with their own metabolisms it becomes clear that they are not separate entities. Cities use nature as their supplier of fuel, food, resource materials and water, and nature also absorbs the waste generated by those cities. The urban population explosion has an ever-increasing influence on what nature is able to deliver. In order to set up an effective and action-oriented urban agenda, we have to redefine the way people lives, moves and works in the city.

In 2005 the hurricane Katrina that destroyed **New Orleans** showed the importance of resilience planning for cities, starting several initiatives and experiments in reimagining urban sustainable protocols. Today the city is a true "resilience lab", having transformed its urban tissue in an inviting and vibrant space, an inspiration for other places savaged by nature's whims and man's mistakes. And the intractability of some its problems — in some cases problems that existed before the storm but have worsened or stagnated since — have made it a magnet for the world's tinkerers, thinkers and doers. Forbes Magazine recently named New Orleans "America's biggest brain magnet." The city saw start-ups launched at a 64 percent higher rate than the national average from 2011 to 2013. Ten years after the hurricane New Orleans has a new urban plan for managing water. "Eighty percent of New Orleans is below sea level" – said Jeff Hebert, New Orleans Chief Resilience Officer – "we had to quickly come up with a plan to intervene and avoid a repeat of what happened in 2005, we tried to emulate initiatives from other major cities, especially plans designed and implemented in Europe."

The *Greater New Orleans Urban Water Plan*, developed in 2013 by Waggonner & Ball Architects, is presented in three main ways: defining an overview of the strategy; proposing different water planning principles through design drawings at various levels; creating an action plan for implementation of the system. The basic components of the plan include making small-scale modifications to canals, parks, wetlands, water systems, monitoring activities and port development areas. Starting from New Orleans's experience, in 2013 the Rockefeller Foundation has launched the challenge **100 Resilient Cities** dedicated to helping cities around the world become more resilient to the physical, social and economic challenges that are a growing part of the 21st century. The initiative supports the adoption and incorporation of a view of resilience that includes not just the shocks – earthquakes, fires, floods, etc. – but also the stresses that weaken the fabric of a city on a day to day or cyclical basis.

In a proactive vision, resilience is the capacity of individuals, communities, institutions, enterprises and services within a city to survive, adapt, and grow no matter what kinds of structural crisis, chronic stresses and acute shocks they experience.

Thus resilience is an enabling device for adaptive, circular and self-sufficient cities for winning the climate change challenge, and for achieving the UN Millennium Sustainable Goals. Advanced ecological policies and plans are able to produce and distribute effectively a "resilience dividend" (Rodin, 2014): a new capital in the economy of the transition toward a decarbonised development, an instrument of urban ecological equalization, and also a multiplier of investments for urban regeneration. The 100RC Initiative wants promote resilient systems sharing and demonstrating certain core characteristics based on five main pillars: a) constant learning, by the ability to internalize past experiences linked with robust feedback loops that sense, provide foresight, and allow new solutions; b) rapid rebound, by the capacity to re-establish function, re-organize, and avoid long-term disruptions; c) limited or "safe" failure, preventing failures from rippling across systems; d) flexibility, by the ability to change, evolve, and adapt to alternative strategies in the face of disaster; e) spare capacity, ensuring that there is a back-up or alternative available when a vital component of a system fails.

Nowadays several cities has been selected for the *100 Resilient Cities Network*, among these Bristol, Dakar, Glasgow, Los Angeles, Mandalay, Medellin, New York, Oakland, Rio De Janeiro, Roma, Rotterdam and San Francisco. And some of them have already appointed a Chief Resilience Officer to lead the charge, to share ideas and to test the potential solutions. The **Oakland** CRO, for example, will lead the city's efforts to prepare for and respond to a number of challenges, from executing earthquake retrofits for 24,000 at-risk multi-family housing units to developing long-term strategies for protecting the city from sea-level rise and intensifying storms, as implemented in the Energy and Climate Action Plan. **Bristol** has plans to create resilient systems—more decentralized, less prone to cascade failure—and will future-proof investment decisions. Bristol is already the most energy and waste-efficient major UK city, and they plan to meet future needs by managing resources even more efficiently. The city aims to empower individuals and communities to help themselves, support capacity building and local-decision making, and protect local amenities. The city is using a systems-led approach to build in capacity, flexibility, safe failure, and constant learning.

New York has more than 520 miles of coastline and more than 8 million residents, nearly 400,000 of whom live in buildings that are physically vulnerable to coastal flooding and sea level rise. Faced with an aging building stock, an expanding 100-year floodplain, and rising costs of insurance, New York City's coastal communities need to be better prepared. The city's efforts to protect its neighborhoods could lead to replicable, cost-effective models for the rest of the world. The Department of City Planning is proposing a zoning text amendment to encourage flood-resilient building construction throughout designated flood zones. The proposed changes are needed in order to remove regulatory barriers that would hinder or prevent the reconstruction of storm-damaged properties. The amendment would enable new and existing buildings to comply with new, higher flood elevations, and to new requirements. Building to these new standards will reduce vulnerability to future floods, as well as help avoid higher flood insurance premiums. But the New York's resilience paradigm shift consists in the winning project of the "Rebuild by Design" competition. The BIG U, drawn by the BIG Team, proposes a protective system around Manhattan from West 54th street south to The Battery and up to East 40th street: 8 continuous miles of low-lying geography that comprise an incredibly dense, vibrant, and vulnerable urban area. The multivalent U consists of multiple but linked design opportunities; each on different scales of time, size and investment; each local neighborhood tailoring its own set of programs, functions, and opportunities. The project proposes that vibrant urban neighborhoods in the floodplain need not be abandoned with increased storms and sea level rise. Instead, these neighborhoods can strategically grow to provide the coastal protection and resilient infrastructure that will address the climate. The Resilient Community Districts proposes that community planning, social resilience, water management, utilities and financial instruments are organized on a district scale as well as an urban scale. Community micro-grids and water management plans create redundancies that decrease the risks posed by increased storms and allow incremental adaptation to climate change. Finally, leveraging local investment into coastal protection, matched with government investment as needed, engages neighbors in developing protective measures that provide for other district needs, and creates tremendous economies of scale that can directly benefit end users.

ECO-CREATIVE DISTRICTS CHALLENGE

Contemporary cities, if we look them with new eyes, possess valuable reserves of resilience, essential to plan and design them as vital organisms in evolution. These cells are resilient to changes (fragments of the agricultural landscape, shreds of infrastructure, neighborhoods in functional recycling, drosscapes and brownfields) and allow the city to take forms more elastic, less resistant to innovation and more adaptive. These reserves are used to enable resilience processes capable of handling a greater number of interacting problems, to engage the plurality of actors and diverse social archipelagos in decisions, and to implement forms of governance able to balance the competition between core and belt cities in an eco-systemic relation. And the cells of resilience from which to reactivate an "urban hyper-metabolism" (Carta, Lino, 2015) more creative, intelligent and ecological focus in marginal areas excluded from the rhetoric of the turbo-development: suburbs in transition, industrial districts restructuring, port areas and railway infrastructures in recycling.

Places – away from the driving centers of the urban model compulsive and consumer of land and resources – have been preserved community values, landscapes and heritage. Values that are precious resources for rethinking a city capable of absorbing the economic crisis, of managing social change and adapting to climate change, redesigning its structure, distributing its centers in reticular forms, resuming relations with the suburban, metropolitan and rural levels.

Especially in the new eco-creative districts – more ecosophic – can restart a city that knows how to call into play its social, territorial and cultural capitals after being recovered from drug addiction drama from that we can call the "subprime urbanism", that has anesthetized the ability to imagine, to plan, to root and to control.
In the new ecological and creative settlements – more resilient, dialogic and sensitive – the cycles of adaptation require a renewed elasticity and flexibility of functions, increased permeability of the spaces and fruitful adaptability of settlements.
On March 2015, the French *Assemblée nationale* approved a new law that mandates all new roofs in commercial zones be partially covered in plants or solar panels. The law produces not only an ecological benefit,

but has some urban effects in transition towards an ecosophic city. First, a green roof benefits a building itself. A layer of plants such as grasses, shrubs, and flowers, provides insulation for the building, reducing the amount of energy needed for heating and cooling. It also creates a green space for building residents to enjoy, something that is often in short supply in cities. Second, green rooftops benefit the entire urban community because they decrease the "heat island" effect. Plantings and solar panels on the tops of new buildings reduce that excess heating effect. The new rooftop law will serve as an example to other countries and comes at a good time for France, which hosted the United Nations' Climate Summit COP 21 in Paris at the end of the 2015. But these should not be addressed as a purely conceptual or spatial problems, but they must be put in relation with the social, economic and technological, today become structural parts of the urban planning, becoming themes / tools / rules for planning a new urban metabolism.

FROM ECOLOGICAL URBANISM TO PROACTIVE ECOLOGY

A major accountability is advisable when it comes to reckoning the scope and size of ecology applied to urban settlement systems, stretching beyond the urban territory. "The city, for all its importance, can no longer be thought of only as a physical artifact; instead, we must be aware of the dynamic relationships, both visible and invisible, that existing among the various domains of a larger terrain of urban as well as rural ecologies. Distinctions between rural and urban contingencies can lead to uncertainties and contradictions – calling for unconventional solutions This regional, holistic approach demonstrates the multi-scalar quality of ecological urbanism" (Mostafavi, 2010). According to this holistic approach, the territorial metabolism should be one of the key planning principles, contributing to reconnect agricultural, residential, industrial, natural, cultural and leisure systems with a view to collaborating and interacting within a mutual exchange of interests between beneficial situations or productive relationships able to influence the organization of space.

We need for a new ethics of convergence of interests will lead the new ecological sustainability, no longer as a frontier to be conquered for land-use planning – as was the case at the end of the last century – but as an operating challenge for a new urban metabolism, which requires to break down sustainability among the dimensions that characterize it.

The political dimension implying, first of all, the development of a culture of understanding and recognition of the other as a fundamental value of relationship, increasingly enriching the common interest through cross-fertilization between different experiences. Local identities are identified as active resources for the development of sociability and community within a sustainable political vision, as opposed to a culture of social polarization that tends to flatten the differences. There is in fact a direct relationship between the growth of the local society, democratic organizations and civic networks with strong bargaining skills in the context of globalization. The political dimension of sustainable development leads us to the implementation of "Lilliputian" strategies to interconnect local societies in order to increase their power to oppose the flattening laws of an exclusively financial globalization, regardless of knowledge and sociality: the global village shall go beyond the global market.

The ecological dimension urges us to endeavour to work at territorial projects ensuring the ecological footprint reduction through urban patterns pursuing the reduction of mobility rate and, at the same time, products' (environmental and cultural, including food) improved quality and uniqueness, reactivation of agricultural activities with a view to multifunctionality and social factors such as the regeneration of the rural and urban land. And, to conclude with, the design of environmental systems and the conditions for their self-reproduction, as they are the main principle of urban settlement systems. Whether it is true, as claimed by David Owen (2009), that the city is – potentially –more sustainable from the ecological point of view than any other settlement forms, the road ahead will inevitably lead to strengthening urban

ecological strategies not as mere norms, but as a political and operating projects, without ruling out the traditional tools of spatial planning. In Europe, following the launch of the new policy to tackle climate change, numerous experiments of plans for urban climate have been launched as a planning response to climate adaptation through a new metabolism.
Chris Reed and Nina-Marie Lister (2014) write that "the past two decades have witnessed a resurgence of ecological ideas and ecological thinking in discussion of urbanism, society, culture and design".

The concept of ecology has moved in favor of more contemporary understandings of dynamic systemic change and the related phenomena of adaptability, resilience, and flexibility. Increasingly these concepts of ecological thought are found useful as heuristics for decision-making generally and as models for cultural production broadly, and for design disciplines in particular.

In *Projective Ecologies* the term "projective" is both important and suggestive: with it, the authors recognize the constructed nature of ecologists' models for the physical and dynamic aspects of the natural world, as well as the limits of science in separating the observer from phenomena observed. So, the processes of which ecology and creativity speak are fundamental to the work of landscape architecture. We need for a powerful "proactive ecology".
The **Diagram n.7** shows the new approach of the proactive ecology in the new challenge for eco-city planning from sustainability to metabolism. Synthesis of the constant interaction between three components: **governance**, which produces the rules, **design** that active projects, and **assessment**, which guides the process. The interaction of these three components, therefore, creates the connection among "economic" components of the **Circular Economy**, "ecosophic" components of the **Urban Metabolism** and "ecological" components of the **Resilient City**.

The **ecosophic** dimension urges the system of public and private actors negotiating the development objectives to be as comprehensive as to ensure that the problems of the poorest social sectors are dealt with, as regards urbanism's collective dimension, enhancing its identification, handling and empowerment. The most interesting expressions of local self-sustainable development are based on the promotion, practices and objectives resulting from the local population's empowerment able to rebalance the relationship between powers (media, economic and political) thus ensuring that communication and participation are based on the legitimacy of the subjects, one of the key aspects of the communication ethics.

The **economic** dimension claims the need to overcome a vision of compliance with econometric parameters linked to a model of development model driven by integrated indicators highlighting the shift from mono-cultural concepts to complex socio-territorial economies ensuring the system's identity preservation, implementing exchange forms that are consistent with the increased assets value. Increasingly intangible economies, based on accessibility rather than ownership, encouraging social inclusiveness rather than segregation, well-being rather than wealth and efficiency rather than consumption are building an effective presence in the vision of the future (Jackson, 2009), requiring care and respect when it comes to the planning approach, that turns into a renewed co-opetition (cooperation + competition) and that reinforce the generative power of the sharing economy.

Finally, the **ecological** dimension provides infrastructure and landscape planning, as well as urbanism and, design with urban settlement patterns promoting the development of the four sustainability by identifying land use thresholds and proposals for the integrated settlements' re-use and re-cycle. Redesigning urban tissues integrated with compatible productive structures requires public space reorganization according to the numerous communities that enliven cities today. We need a re-boot of the city generated by the redesign of the urban fabric in integration with the new micro and nano manufacturing, with makers and fablabs, able to generate the reorganization of urban space - increasingly shared - in relation to multiple communities that animate the city today. But above all, the sustainable territorial dimension needs creative urban planning: from local development and the gateway cities networks, to the virtual digital cities where the interaction of many collective, multi-cultural and multi-ethnic intelligences produces new communities.

ECOLOGY AND ENERGY ALLIANCE: ALGAE POWER

Around the world there are many good practices and experiments in progress, but it is mainly in France that the challenge of eco-city has become the main policy of urban armature based on the Ecocités to start strategic processes designed to transform the spatial form, the economy and the image of the city within a new urban metabolism and to activate a stronger ecological cycle. According to the *Grenelle Environnement* principles, in 2008 the French Government launched the Sustainable City Action Plan adopting an innovative approach to urban planning based on local communities and compliance with development sustainability project. Neither a set of rules or high-performance technological equipment are sufficient per se: green living is the sum of the states of equilibrium of each individual within its environment. It's a collective balance that even a single deviant behaviour can jeopardize. It needs a new alliance among ecology and housing, transport, energy, social behaviours.

In the alliance between ecology and energy the algae are the leading actors of ecological architectures and subject of several trials. In **Hamburg** will built the world's first algae-powered building. Designed by Arup and Splitterwerk for the IBA 2013, the BIQ House is covered in bio-reactive louvers that enclose the algae: these louvers allow the algae to survive and grow faster than they would otherwise while also providing shade for the interior of the building. The bio-reactors not only produce biomass that can subsequently be harvested, but they also capture solar thermal heat – and both energy sources can be used to power the building. This means that photosynthesis is driving a dynamic response to the amount of solar shading required, while the micro-algae growing in the glass louvres provide a clean source of renewable energy.

Another example of eco-energy building is the MediaTIC Building in **Barcelona**, designed by Cloud-9 architect's office. The building is in the shape of a cube and formed by large iron beams covered in a plastic coating of inflatable bubbles (EFTE skin), which offer glimpses of the fluorescent structure of the building. The attractive covering also has a functional utility as a way of regulating light and temperature, primarily preventing 114 tons of CO_2 a year from escaping from the building, and offering a 20% saving on climate control. The intelligent skin is activated using pneumatic mechanisms thanks to luxometer sensors, energy independent, that automatically and independently activate the chamber inflation and deflation devices according to how much solar energy there is.

These are the first of a new generation of intelligent and ecologic buildings: living buildings that respond and adapt to the conditions around them. In the ecologic city buildings will function as a living organism in its own right, reacting to the local environment and engaging with the users within.

The responsibility for development metamorphosis and the commitment to re-imagining urbanism from shared visions and addresses shall be implemented through a new route leading to the island, searching for methods and practices based on a few key points, that is the new ethic of responsibility for decision-makers and a new agenda for urbanists and planners.

Above all should be included new creative city sensibilities and paradigms within town planning in order to enhance urban talents, re-cycling urbanism paradigms in the practice of brownfield areas' creative design, urban shrinkage paradigms as land project beyond consumption and the smartness ones, thus renewing the water-energy-waste cycles and managing digital and mobility networks in a sustainable way. Furthermore, the paradigm of post-carbon economy, driver of innovation and investment multiplier, of urban agriculture as activator of new metabolisms and finally of infrastructure retrofitting as adequate intervention method on inefficient cities need to be considered.

If gardening is the 21st century urban mainstream, we assist at the raise of "cyber-gardening", that's all about applying the latest technologies to produce our food. London-based design office EcoLogicStudio has developed a new agro-urban prototype for algae cultivation — a digital design project that combines urbanism, food manufacturing and ecology. The hanging algae garden is self-reliant and consists of micro- and macro-algal organisms. The system is equipped with ambient light, sensing technologies and a virtual interface. Observations, data and results of the experiment can be tracked online. People passing by can also contribute to the project by breathing into a tube. This way the algae are being supplied with CO_2.

Algae cultivation could offer new opportunities for economic development in the Sweden's **Österlen** region, where the population is aging and fishing activities are diminishing. Algae, as raw material for food, fuel and chemicals, can provide new jobs to farmers and fishermen in this coastal region. The cultivation of algae can also contribute to the production of bio-energy in Sweden, but the project inquires the applicability to larger algae landscapes. This kind of urban agriculture makes people think about sustainable systems, integrating the rural and urban landscape of the future.

Rethinking human settlements sustainability is the goal dell'*Algal Carbon Conversion Project*, a three-year project that will see the construction of a photobioreactor (financed by 19 million Canadian dollars) near **Bonnyville**, in the central-eastern province of Alberta. The project will demonstrate the "economic sustainability" of the photobioreactor that dosing carbon dioxide, heat, waste water plants and algae oil would transform the mixture into biofuel and natural fertilizers for agriculture. "For each ton of algae - said Joy Romero, vice president of technology development of Canadian Natural Resources - we could eliminate 1.8 tons of CO2, release into the environment 1.3 tons of oxygen and produce 0.3 tons of biofuel and 0.7 tons of biomass. With two plants you might get to eliminate 1.5 million tons of CO2: how to remove 300.000 vehicles from the streets".

URBAN AGRICULTURE INITIATIVES

For centuries, agricultural developments have been determined the European landscape. Intensification, mechanization, expansion and industrialization of arable farming have changed the landscape, decoupling it from the urban physiognomy and physiology. In particular the peri-urban agriculture has disappeared, compress between the need of large cultivation areas and the sprawl of urbanisation. Agriculture has lost its landscape, civic and social dimension, often slipping on the margins of industrial production and the farms have disappeared from the urban horizon.

Food has been an urban product since long. The United Nations Development Program (UNDP) estimated that urban agriculture delivers up to one fifth of the food produced today. Advanced and sensitive city planning understands the link between the resources (energy, water, sunlight, carbon etc.) urban agriculture and livestock. Urban agriculture is a concept that restores our common knowledge of a cyclic system of life and its necessities. By 2050 up to 80% of the earth's population will reside in urban centers. Until then human population will increase by about 3 billion, applying conservative estimates. If food is to be consumed and produced in as inefficient way as today we will need further arable land the size of Brazil by 2050. Over 70 % of land area suitable for farming is used for crop production. Most of this production is for fodder for animals not for human food, this happens in a time when grazing on natural land is more and more rare even though it produces both biodiversity and a landscape with high nature values. Urban farming is safer, more local and with less/no input of unnatural pesticides. Products from urban agriculture are in most cases probably already ecologically sound in some perspectives. In this field a leader is Plantagon, a Stockholm based international enterprise that has engineered an innovative urban greenhouse. In **Linköping**, Sweden, the first Plantagon Greenhouse broke ground in 2012. A new type of greenhouse for vertical farming, an international Centre of Excellence for Urban Agriculture and a demo-plant for Swedish clean-tech and a climate-smart way to use excess heating and CO_2 from industries. The Plantagon greenhouse, developed together with Sweco, is designed for vertical agriculture of vegetables in urban areas, and it will be an integrated solutions for energy, excess heat, waste, CO_2 and water. Not least, it will be a new landmark for the people in Linköping to enjoy.

Urban agriculture can reflect varying levels of economic and social development. In first northern experiments it often takes the form of a social movement for sustainable communities, where organic growers, foodies, and "locavores" form social networks founded on a shared ethos of nature and community holism.

These networks had evolved when received formal institutional support, becoming integrated into local town planning as a "transition town" movement for sustainable urban development. In the developing south experiences, instead, food security, nutrition, and income generation are key motivations for the practice. In either case, more direct access to fresh vegetables, fruits, and meat products through urban agriculture can improve food security and food safety and reactivate the agricultural urban cycles.
In Wyoming (USA) the town of **Jackson Hole** has launched a new initiative called Vertical Harvest — a multi-storey greenhouse built on the side of a parking lot — hoping that one of the world's few vertical farms can help feed the town with tomatoes, herbs, and microgreens. Using hydroponics, Vertical Hole will be capable of producing over 37,000 pounds of greens, 4,400 pounds of herbs, and 44,000 pounds of tomatoes. The vertical farm offers the same growing areas as 23

acres of traditional farmland, and has a fraction of the environmental impact, using 90 percent less water and 100 percent fewer pesticides than traditional farming. Funded partially through a successful Kickstarter campaign and set up in collaboration with Jackson Hole's town authorities, initiative is also a social provider, offering jobs at the vertical farm to people with developmental disabilities, who will be planting and harvesting the crops.

Urban farming, however, is not just an architectural or technological experimentation but, in the Augmented City, becomes a key component of its structural resilience: renewed cycle of its metabolism.

Accompanied by an exceptional testimonial, Michelle Obama, the U.S. urban agriculture has become not only a common practice in small towns or in the interstitial spaces of the city, but a strategy for cities in transition: Detroit, Cleveland, Portland, Austin, Boston, Chicago, Seattle, Baltimore, Milwaukee, Minneapolis are ten American cities that lead the way with urban agriculture ordinances. **San Diego** is currently an example of how urban agriculture can be a political priority, a pivotal project for spatial, social and environmental regeneration in the disrepaired districts of the city, included in the planning rules, so as to provide the most disadvantaged social groups with accessibility, production and consumption of local agricultural products. In 2010, the San Diego General Plan was awarded by the American Planning Association for having introduced specific categories of urban land use such as the Farmers Markets and Retail Farms — thus promoting urban agriculture as a channel of community — common backyard gardens allowing citizens to benefit from self-production of healthier food or to start direct-sale microbusinesses in the residual interstices of the changing city. But is **New York** the city that is becoming a leader in transforming urban farming into a structural component of its future, spreading community vegetable gardens, especially in Brooklyn with a true "back-to-the-land" boom, which produce fresh and healthy food for local communities of the entire metropolitan area.

Urban agriculture is an increasingly global trend due to the benefits that it can bring to urban environments. The range of benefits is very diverse, from environmental (stormwater mitigation, air purification, nutrient recycling, urban cooling etc.) or social (food security, education, recreation, physical activity, improvement in healthy eating, improved social cohesion etc.) to economical (income generation, added real estate value, supplying niche markets etc.).

In Europe, there are a lot of projects and experiments about the urban farms, but some of them are more relevant for rethinking and redesigning the urban environment to improve the city resilience. In the context of the Netherlands, a highly industrialized country, food security is not currently the main motivation behind the practice, but rather the effort to increase awareness of the importance of local food and its impacts. **Rotterdam** is a pioneering city, hosting more than 100 active initiatives besides the allotment complexes. However, most of these initiatives are small and do not have significant impacts on a citywide scale. Rotterdam has a large potential surface that can potentially be converted to UA initiatives. Grasslands and derelict lands without contamination issues amount to 3900 ha and there are 906 ha of suitable flat roofs. Even converting a small percentage of these surfaces would have considerable impacts in the city. Many plots scattered around Rotterdam can benefit from the added functionality brought about by urban agriculture.

After the success of participation and results of the Réinventer Paris, in 2016 Mayor Anne Hidalgo launched another challenge to make **Paris** a more resilient, creative and collaborative city: Le Paris Culteurs, an opensource competition for transforming 46 sites for a total of 5.5 hectares into vegetable epicenters of urban and human regeneration of spaces and communities. Today, with 33 graduated projects *Les Paris Culteurs* is one of the most interesting experiment in transition from urban horticulture to farming urbanism. An Augmented City based on a green archipelago of urban gardens, greenhouses, garden roofs, edible walls and green infrastructure becomes the new framework of the next city, connecting resilience with production, open collaboration with adaptive and incremental strategies.

Also **London** is acting to be the worldwide urban farming capital, with a lot of experiments and projects. One of them is the *London Capital Growth* initiative, a partnership between London Food Link, the Mayor of London Boris Johnson, and the Big Lottery's Local Food Fund. It supported the creation of 2012 new community food growing spaces across London by the end of 2012. Capital Growth offers practical help, training and support to people wanting to grow their own food, whether at home, on an allotment or as part of a community group. The initiative starts from the *London Food Strategy* for a new model of social housing, able to improve a more sustainable and cohesive communities. Where there is interest among residents, urban food growing projects can be an excellent way of contributing to these goals. In the filed of this strategy a particular relevance has the *Capital Bee* initiative, that has established seven training sites for 75 beekeepers in schools, community centers and housing estates. It encourages Londoners to help make the city bee-friendly by growing their own food and bee-friendly flowers in their gardens. Finally, the initiative asks people to renounce the use of pesticides by buying organic products and using them in their own gardens. The London Food Strategy "Healthy & Sustainable Food for London" (2006) sets a vision to 2016 and outlines 5 key strategic objectives: a) to improve Londoners' health and reduce health inequalities via the food they eat; b) to reduce the negative environmental impacts of London's food system; c) to support a vibrant food economy; d) to celebrate and promote London's food culture e) to develop London's food security. The "urban food" philosophy lies at the heart of London spatial planning systems, epitomised by the London Plan, an evolving but nonetheless dynamic resource for ensuring a better quality of life for everyone. Improved food access, especially in deprived areas, is central to this and spatial planning offers an opportunity to give expression to health inequalities and other shortcomings in the capital's food supply by ensuring they have a deserved profile in a host of policy areas. Spatial planning should encompass the development of on-farm processing facilities, the provision of sub-regional food distribution systems, the protection of street markets, farmers' markets and specialist markets, the maintenance of the High Street, tackling food 'deserts' and a host of other food-related issues.

The London Food Strategy has produced several initiatives and projects. One of these is **Edible Hackney**, promoted by Mikey Tomkins, a beekeeper, who has a vision for the neighborhood as a heartland of food production. Over two years he mapped a 25 hectares area, marking up both where food could be produced and where it already was: the result is Edible Hackney Map. It's not an urban farm in the traditional sense but a grassroots reclamation of space for food growing. The project translates ideas of "local food" into tangible, interactive and playful stories, reconnecting people to a place through local food-growing. The map charts what could be next, a cartography of what i seal mixed with future hopes, marking out the city's potential for sustainable living.

London is also becoming one of the world capitals of **Treeconomics**, an innovative theory that reveals the economic value of the "urban forests". An open-source software called **i-Tree** maps city trees and calculates the financial value of the "ecosystem services" they provide. It's estimated that in London there are about 8 million trees. While street trees are a visible green stamp on a city, 70% of the urban forest is found in private gardens and places such as railway embankments, cemeteries and golf courses. Trees that are close to buildings reduce air conditioning in summer, and even heating bills in winter – small effects that become extremely valuable in a big city.

From the pioneering guerrilla initiatives or social horticulture the urban agriculture is an innovative metropolitan strategy and an effective design tool for reimagining and planning the future resilient cities.

Munich with the Agropolis Project by Jörg Schroeder of the Hannover University has launched a metropolitan food strategy aimed to "rediscover harvest for everyday urban life". According to the London Food Strategy the Munich's strategy could significantly improve on the health of citizens and reduce health inequalities, reduce the negative environmental impacts of the current food system, initiate and support a vibrant food economy, celebrate and promote Munich's food culture, and improve overall food quality and develop food security.

The new role of urban agriculture has become an essential topic in discussions dealing with the goals of sustainability, climate change challenge and energy saving. Due to a growing global demand for food as a result of population increase and consequent decrease of landmass, the demand for agricultural land is growing. In response to the climate change an increase in agricultural land is foreseen to strongly benefit areas like central Europe, where soil amelioration suddenly becomes significant.

Schroeder wrote that «inner city areas tend to be some relevant degrees warmer - this could make them attractive cultivation areas, which would in turn alleviate and balance the inner city climate. The widespread demand for healthy food as part of a healthy lifestyle is growing; not only regarding bio-products but also for low cost self-sufficiency. According to these factors the role of agriculture and food supply will be reevaluated within the urban development of Munich». Agropolis' first step is a temporary farm in Freiham, the next big development area of Munich. Freiham will be transformed into a building site for approximately 30 years. The aim of the proposal is to convey an impression of this transformation by allocating a consistent temporary agrarian use to future building sites, as it is already common and effective in Munich. Excavators and tractors in the area will not displace each other but through their coexistence will generate a new urban model: Agropolis. In a sequence of actions this temporary use can become a catalyst to integrate agriculture and food supply into Munich's urban development - in order to consolidate and strengthen urban density. The ritual of bringing your own food to the beer garden will be further developed into a rediscovery of harvesting as an everyday urban activity. Commercial and self supply urban agriculture will explore unused spaces like roofs, facades, gaps, and niches. The upgrading of house gardens, balconies and community gardens follows the motto "strengthen density and intensify use". Agropolis' networking, interaction and rediscovery of fundamental parts of a food system is a relevant part of the new urban map. Awareness will be raised through a number of different installations such as salt spreading machines to distribute seeds, billboards set up on Ludwigsstrasse and temporary agricultural plantations integrated in parks and public spaces. Agropolis' aim is not to create images, but more to perceive the movements of harvesting, being part of everyday life as a projectual motor for the production of urban space.

Today the urban farming movement has now its poetics and visual imagery: *Edible City* is a 55 minute documentary film released in 2015 that introduces a diverse cast of people who are challenging the paradigm of our broken food system. The film digs deep into their unique perspectives and transformative work, finding inspirational, grass-roots solutions based on growing local food systems and economies.

Through several declarations, many good practices and breakthrough pioneering initiatives (Sommariva, 2014), urban agriculture is no longer a planning utopia, is no longer a sensitive approach to urban development, is no longer an ecological alternative to the consumption of soil, but it is a structural component of the resilience of cities, it's a planning device of the urban ecology and it's a design tool of the Augmented City as a renewed "pasture and nurturer of society" – as Plato wrote in *Politeia*.

ENERGY AND FOOD AS URBAN RESOURCES

01

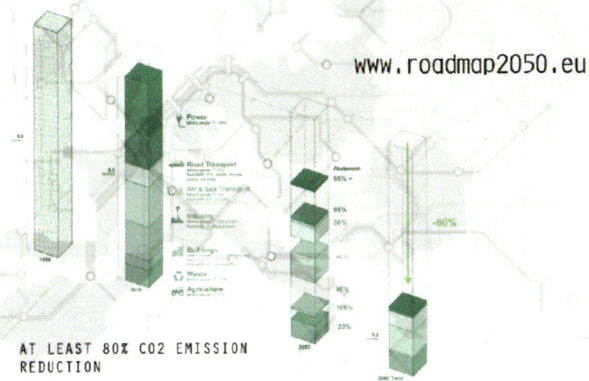

Roadmap 2050

a practical guide to a prosperous, low carbon Europe

www.roadmap2050.eu

AT LEAST 80% CO2 EMISSION REDUCTION

01-02. Europe RoadMap 2050 for a low-carbon economy is one of the most important political/technical document for a more resilient Europe. The Roadmap suggests that, by 2050, the EU should cut its emissions to 80% below 1990 levels through domestic reductions alone. It sets out milestones which form a cost-effective pathway to this goal - reductions of the order of 40% by 2030 and 60% by 2040. It also shows how the main sectors responsible for Europe's emissions - power generation, industry, transport, buildings and construction, as well as agriculture - can make the transition to a low-carbon economy most cost-effectively. Europe will be change from the existing grid phasing based on backbone to a new decarbonized grid power shared distribution.

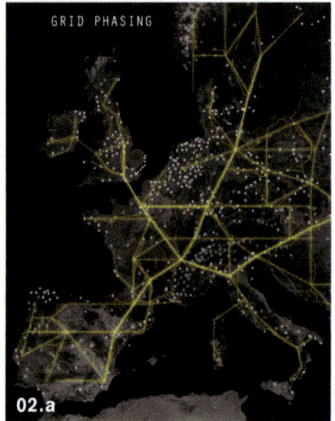

02.a GRID PHASING

02.b 2050 EUROPEAN ENERGY GRID

03.

03. Beddington Zero Energy Development (BedZED) is an environmentally friendly housing development in Hackbridge, London, England. It was designed by the architect Bill Dunster to be carbon neutral, protecting the environment and supporting a more sustainable lifestyle. The project was also pioneering by being the first construction project where a local authority sold land at below market value to make sustainable economically development viable. The district has 82 homes and 1,405 square metres of work space.

04. The **Sonnenschiff Solar City** in Freiburg (Germany) is very much net positive project. Designed by Rolf Disch, the Sonnenschiff (Solar Ship) and Solarsiedlung (Solar Village) emphasize power production from the start by smartly incorporating a series of large rooftop solar arrays that double as sun shades. The buildings are also built to Passivhaus standards, which allows the project to produce four times the amount of energy it consumes. The project started out as a vision for an entire community — the medium-density project balances size, accessibility, green space, and solar exposure. In all, 52 homes make up a neighborhood anchored to Sonnenschiff, a mixed-use residential and commercial building that emphasizes livability with a minimal footprint. Advanced technologies like phase-change materials and vacuum insulation significantly boost the thermal performance of the building's wall system.

05. Uneven Growth by Superpool is a research for tactics for Resilient Post-Urban Development. Turkey is currently one of the fastest-growing economies in Europe. At 14 million inhabitants and a yearly growth rate of 3.5 percent, Istanbul has fully benefited from this economic boom. Starting in the 1960s, its rapid urbanization has had three main phases: gecekondus squatter villages; post-gecekondus' additional building rights; and mass housing since the 1990s. Unlike earlier "self-building" phases, the recent mass housing is organized predominantly through the Housing Development Agency of Turkey, Toplu Konut daresi Ba kanlı ı (TOKI), and it employs a single urban typology: gated complexes of repetitive tower clusters on open land. TOKI development parallels the emergence of a new middle class in Istanbul for whom a TOKI flat is part of a dream of car and house ownership, even if this brings social isolation, long hours in traffic, and long-term debt. This deeply

indebted middle class is also prone to be the most vulnerable during periods of recession. In the face of continuing political, economic, and ecological uncertainties, and the rising costs of energy, TOKI inhabitants have to become more resilient.

Kolektif birlikçi Toplum Olu umu / The Collective and Collaborative Agency (KITO), is a proposal for a post-urban development initiative that uses open-source, citizen-driven R-Urban regeneration to transform TOKI complexes. KITO works at different scales and levels of resilient action to retrofit spaces, equipment, services, and institutions. KITO's collective interaction is facilitated via KITO'da, an online network that creates an alternative economy, assigning value to local actions and empowering people to make, give, share, and save energy, services, goods, knowledge, and skills. Instead of consuming the city, residents share in its production.

06. R-URBAN is a participative strategy for development, practices and networks of local resilience elaborated by Atelier d'Architecture Autogérée. The strategy explores as such alternatives to the current models of living, producing and consuming in cities, suburbs and rural areas. It draws on the active involvement of citizen in initiating collaborative practices and creating solidarity networks, closing cycles between production and consumption, operating changes in lifestyles, acting ecologically at the level of everyday life. R-URBAN will be developed as a pilot project over a four-year period on a number of sites in Colombes, a city located in the northwestern suburbs of Paris. The project will gradually create a network around three Units, each with complementary urban functions, and will bring together emerging citizen projects in the logic of resilience. The EcoHab unit consists of 7 houses mixing social housing, home ownership and residencies of artists, students and researchers. EcoHab will have an experimental character and the construction must associate self-construction and training. Halfway between co-housing and cooperatives, the focus of this residential unit is to: a) experiment with ecological living and living (shared services and spaces, water recycling, intensive vegetable gardens, renewable energies, etc.); b) rationally manage natural resources, including a model for other housing, to reduce domestic consumption; c) constitute an archive of knowledge and know-how of urban ecology and create, in the medium term, a place to share resilient practices.

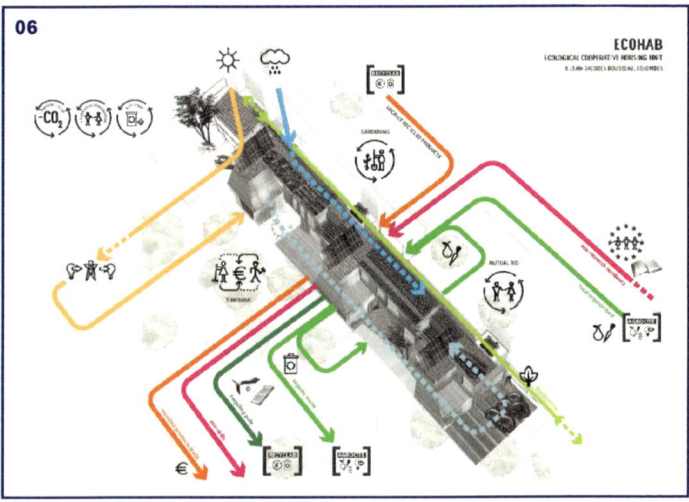

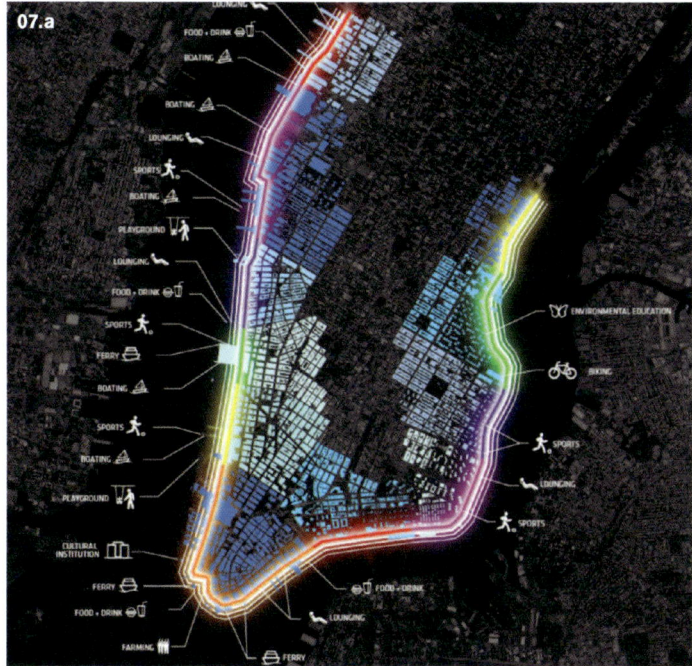

07. A vision to protect post-Sandy Manhattan against future superstorms, Bjarke Ingels Group's (BIG) "**Dry Line**" seeks to form a continuous storm barrier around lower Manhattan by transforming underutilized waterfront spaces into a "protective ribbon" of public parks and amenities. Though ambitious, the project is not impossible; it was one of six winners in the US' Rebuild by Design competition that is envisioning ways New York can protect its edge. BIG's proposal, The BIG U, is rooted in the firm's signature concepts of social infrastructure and hedonistic sustainability. It envisions a 10-mile protective system that encircles Manhattan, protecting the city from floods and storm water while simultaneously providing public realms specific to the needs of the city's diverse communities. The Big U is a protective system that encircles Manhattan, responding to the needs and concerns of the island's diverse communities. Stretching from West 57th Street south to The Battery and up to East 42nd Street, the Big U protects 10 continuous miles of low-

07.b

lying geography that comprise an incredibly dense, vibrant, and vulnerable urban area. The team's approach is rooted in the two concepts of social infrastructure and hedonistic sustainability. The Big U not only shields the city against floods and storm water; it provides social and environmental benefits to the community, and fosters an improved public realm. The team envisions three compartments that function independently to provide flood protection. Each compartment comprises a physically discrete flood-protection zone that can be isolated from flooding in adjacent zones. At the same time, each presents opportunities for integrated social and community planning. The compartments work in unison to protect and enhance the city, yet each compartment's proposal is designed to stand on its own.

08. Resilience is the new battlefield for the most innovative companies. **New Google's Headquarters,** in Mountain View, is a 316,000 sqm campus by Bjarke Ingels Group and Thomas Heatherwick. The proposal comprises lightweight and flexible block structures which can be moved to accommodate for future use. Large translucent canopies cover each site, controlling the internal climate while letting in daylight and ventilation, and dissolving the boundaries between the built and natural environment. In Seattle the Amazon's Spheres by NBBJ architects are the new office buildings as a massive spherical greenhouse-like structure capable of housing multiple forms of plant life as well as mature trees. The building will put ecological active devices in Seattle's urban landscape.

08.a

08.b

ENVELOPE

HUMAN SCALE

NATURE

08.c

09. The London based ecoLogicStudio, (Claudia Pasquero and Marco Poletto) has proposed a new vision of future bio-digital architecture powered by microalgae organisms as part of the Future Food District project, curated by Carlo Ratti Associati at the central crossroads of the EXPO site. This vision is about to become reality as a large **Urban Canopy** roof in the central square of the district. The 1:1 scale mock-up presented in Milan prefigures the world's first bio-digital canopy integrating micro-algal cultures and real time digital cultivation protocols on a unique architectural system. The exceptional properties of microalgae organisms are enhanced by their cultivation within a custom designed 3 layers ETFE cladding system. The flows of energy, water and CO_2 are therefore regulated to respond and adjust to weather patterns and visitors' movements. As the sun shines more intensively algae would photosynthesise and grow thus reducing the transparency of the canopy and increasing its shading potential; since this process is driven by the biology of micro-algae is inherently responsive and adaptive; visitors will benefit from this natural shading property while being able to influence it in real-time; their presence will trigger electro valves to alter the speed of algal flow through the canopy provoking an emergent differentiation across the space. In any moment in time the actual transparency, colour and shading potential of the canopy will be the product of this complex set of relationships among climate, micro-algae, visitors and digital control systems.

YOU ARE HUNGRY: AN EDIBLE MAP OF SOUTH HACKNEY

Feeding the 1,425 residents of South Hackney, London, using the 25 hectares of land that surrounds them*

10. Mapping an Edible Urban Hackney investigates how much food can be grown on 25 hectares of south Hackney. The map is a way to visualise the sometime complex idea of urban food growing, within everyday spaces of city. Just what does an edible landscape look like? The map is therefore a vision, a provocation and an invitation to participate to making edible city space. Mikey Tomkins, an expert on urban agriculture and a bee-keeper with hives on the roof of a nearby building, produced the map called Edible Hackney, which imagines how the streets and estates of a small area of E8 could be turned to food production. He drew beehives on the roof of the 17-storey building and placed raised beds of vegetables and fruit trees around its base. The garages on the far side of the road became mushroom farms, and London Fields was the venue for an annual festival of local produce. The map offers a beguiling vision of a district recently ravaged by riots, and yet it isn't entirely wishful thinking. In total, Tomkins has counted 26 different kinds of fruit and vegetable within the area defined by his map, though he doesn't claim that it's possible, or desirable, for Hackney's residents to become entirely self-sufficient. The Growing Communities, a Hackney-based collective who produces veg boxes from Hackney-grown production, is a perfect example of the practice that Tomkins would like to encourage, for it specialises in the kind of salads and leafy greens that are best produced "close to market".

11. The **Agropolis project** is the winner of the 2009 Open Scale competition in Munich, developed by an interdisciplinary team of architects, urbanists and landscape architects led by Jörg Schroeder. The plan suggests to re-introduce urban agriculture into the metropolitan region, promoting regional green networks. Each inhabitant of Munich actually would need 2.040 sqm. of arable land and grassland for the annual food supply - clearly not possible within city borders. Agropolis München therefore invites Munich to a metropolitan food strategy that articulates a sustainable food economy from production to meals, from farms and gardens to markets and restaurants, creating real place and real time experiences. Focussing on the promotion of self-supply and sustainable use of soil within the city, harvesting can become a renewed part of urban life. The development area Freiham (for 20.000 future inhabitants) is suggested by Agropolis as case study for new approaches to rural-urban transformation processes. The period of 30 years puts the not yet built fallow lands inside Freiham development into consideration; temporary agricultural use - including a new form of urban farm - of the Freiham area, as well as persistent elements, can integrate urban agriculture into sustainable development. Public and private spaces would be preconfigured with 7000 fruit trees, vegetable production and self-supply are embedded into ongoing planning processes. Urban agriculture draws visitors and users and adds to the quality of life and recreational value for the already built housing estates and the whole city, implementing a persistent brand for the up until now marginal Freiham. Already conceived by Munich city planning as sustainable city regarding energetic issues, a further impressive layer of sustainable development will be added with the Agropolis brand.

11.a

11.b

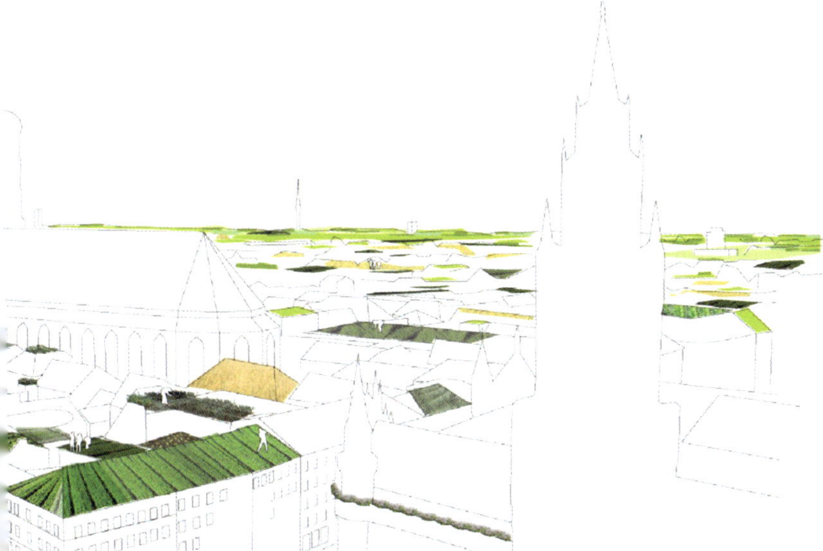

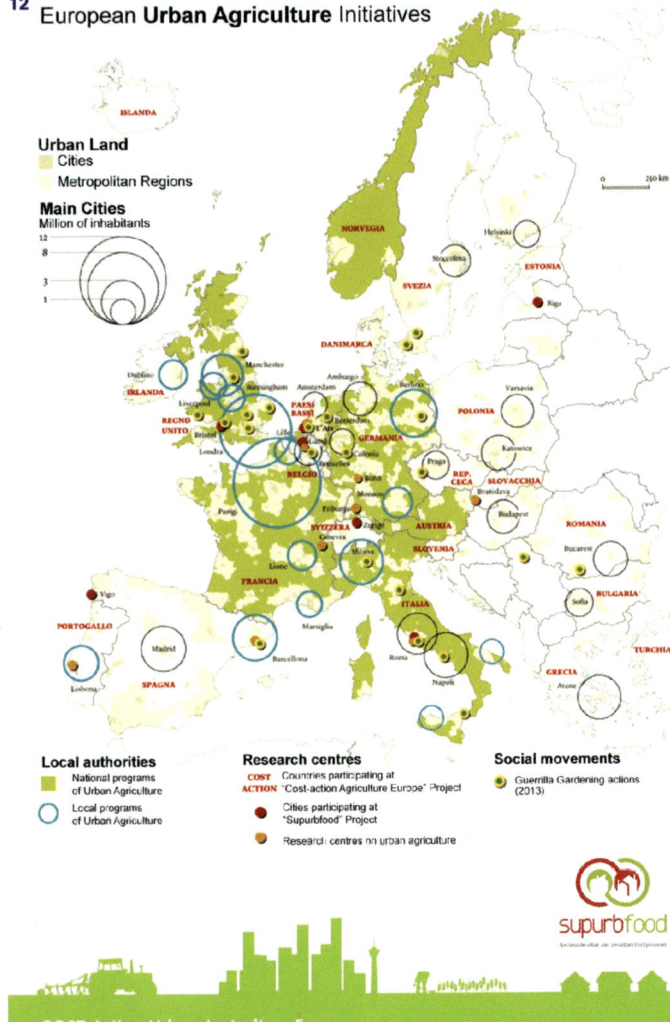

12. Urban Agriculture plays a key role in two global challenges: urbanization and food security. It can provide an important contribution to sustainable, resilient urban development and the creation and maintenance of multifunctional urban landscapes. In the globally emerging research field of Urban Agriculture, a European approach to the subject needs to be created. It has to integrate the unique European context regarding its urban and landscape pattern, the important role of the Common Agriculture Policy (CAP) and the needs of the European society. The **COST-Action-Urban Agriculture Europe** (UAE) will initiate the definition of this European approach on the basis of existing research projects and reference regions in the partner countries. More than 120 researchers from 61 Universities and research institutions in 21 European countries are participating in COST UAE and are contributing their knowledge on Urban Agriculture. The outcomes of the Action will help to focus future research on urban agriculture, modify the CAP and stimulate private and public activities in urban agriculture projects and planning. The Action will use an innovative approach crossing bottom-up and top-down methods, using the method of research by design and creating interfaces between the three methods. By working in close cooperation with regional stakeholders from the domains of urban development and agriculture the Action contributes to sustainable, resilient territorial development in Europe and aims for leadership in research on urban agriculture in developed countries. At the end of the project the final recommendations to regional, national and European institutions were proposed by researchers involved in the project: a) recognize urban agriculture as a cultural and social resource for quality of urban life and wellbeing; b) recognize urban agriculture as a driving force for innovation in the whole agricultural sector; c) raise awareness for urban agriculture and its special conditions, potentials and demands; d) promote research and strategic development on urban agriculture.

Today, after the first leisure-based generation and after the second one based on cultural and services investments, a new paradigm about urban waterfronts regeneration should guide us. The third generation in waterfront planning and design have to be creativity-driven, able to produce a whole regeneration force for the city competitiveness, smartness and quality, contributing at the urban fluidity.

8. FLUID

THE FLUID CITY
Porosity and fluidity as projective paradigms

from separation and conflict

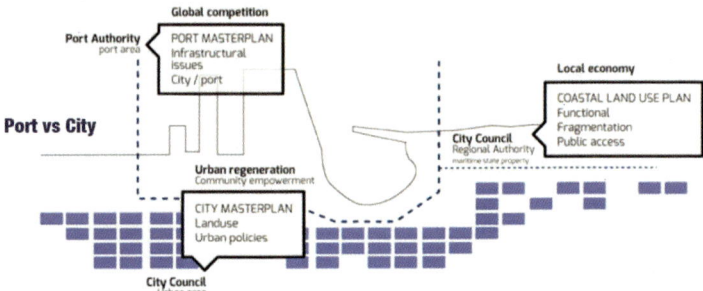

to integration and interaction

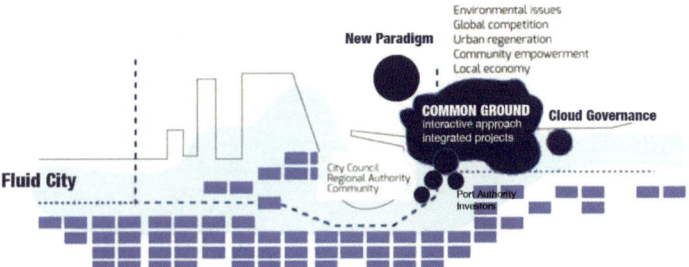

THE FLUID CITY PARADIGM

Urban waterfronts are today one of the most prolific variants of augmented cities: fluid and hybrid places where resources, opportunities, aspirations and ambitions of cities are translated into visions, new relations and projects. The creative port city is capable of reactivating new fluid metabolism, generating new architectural forms and producing new landscapes. The permanent flows of urban culture, grounding on the waterfront, are capable to fuel huge relational networks, making cities more dynamic, communicative and competitive. The most important implication of waterfront regeneration is that this particular area should be addressed as a structural and strategic element of the city as a whole. Enforcing the fluidity as a characteristic of the contemporary cities. One of the inevitable consequences of tightly inter-woven relations among cities, ports and coastal areas is that tools of intervention used on urban waterfronts must be capable of intercepting, interpreting and transforming the entire city and not be restricted purely to areas along the coast. Rising to the challenge of the urban waterfront as a spark of urban regeneration demands targeted efforts to create the sensation of a waterfront not so much as a physical location but more in the form of flexible, porous, liquid aspects of the whole city: what I defined the Fluid City paradigm (Carta, Ronsivalle, 2016). So fluid city planning and design need to answer the following question: in order to reduce the vulnerability and improve the resilience should cities place restrictions on their built-up areas or try to find new paths of organising and using the water zones? How can they reduce vulnerability based on climate change, landscape characteristics and the intrinsic functioning of urban society? Considering architecture and urbanism advanced standards and regulations, adaption and reversible uses, technological research and smart innovation, how are urban regeneration projects being structured and how do they help reimagine the city from a sustainable and resilient development perspective? What kind of landscape and urban redevelopments can help mitigate flood risk reconciling the environmental imperatives of sustainable development with the economic tasks of competitive growth? (Terrin, 2014).

These specific questions call for cross-cutting approaches in order to bypass oppositions, conflicts and sectorial policy barriers and work in a mutually beneficial way. Waterfronts, therefore, are more than straightforward urban contexts, they are better described as structural components of cities, frequently part of a harbour clusters and the focus of combined action: they are fluid eco-communities requiring wide-ranging strategic action so as to fully exploit cultural, tourist and productive capitals. European port cities are also important portals providing access to imposing production platforms between the Atlantic and the Mediterranean, between the Americas and Asia, and as a consequence must be capable of establishing new functions which go beyond the stereotypical images of marginalization and degradation, so often associated with ports.

Today a new paradigm of knowledge/action on urban waterfronts should guide us, and we could define it the third generation in waterfront planning, after the first leisure-based generation (i.e. Baltimora) and after the second one based on cultural and services investments (i.e. Barcelona). The third generation in waterfront planning and design have to be creativity-driven, able to produce a whole regeneration force for the city competitiveness, smartness and quality, contributing at the urban fluidity,

From the urban creative dividend factors – as described in Chapter 5 – we could extract some fluid city's guidelines for decision-making and planning on third generation waterfronts development. These guidelines are structured around seven principles that decline the creative action for urban innovation based on the relation with the following criteria: a) the **identity** principle, typically displaying deep cultural stratification of waterfront identity resources, coupled with the willingness and ability of institutions and technicians to optimize such resources, in addition to a population which is aware of the importance of interaction and its active role in the transformation process. These elements are most frequently encountered in historic waterfronts, places where a sense of belonging is rooted in both space and time, along with an increased awareness of cultural values;

b) the **economic sustainability** principle, which calls for a pre-existing, solid economic base – either internal or to be set up in financial partnerships – to activate and maintain waterfront regeneration within a context of policies and regulations aimed at facilitating their completion. In those areas we have to improve the use of public-private partnership tools or business improvement districts can be put in place for setting up some incentive to encourage new business into the area;

c) the **potentiality** principle appraises coastal area experiencing an imbalance between the top-level potential envisaged or recognized by analysts, planners, artists and entrepreneurs and sets this against its current circumstances and decision-making trends. This imbalance acts as a sort of transformer, converting potential energy into the kinetic one needed for regeneration. Just think of the extraordinary reserves of opportunity possessed by port districts with large tracts of brownfield sites and factories, just waiting to be transformed into incubators of activity, into developer of smartness or to provide the necessary space for large-scale service facilities;

d) the **dynamism** principle hands back the know-how, competence and tools needed to set creative process in motion and produce future transformation in the fields of culture, science and technology. Think of the enormous contribution made by cultural associations or micro-enterprises which forge the very nerve centre of the new socio-economic framework of town planning. Another great, dynamic resource is the presence of communities of artists, creative and talents taking up residence in port disused areas; redefining functions, opening galleries, setting up theatre programmes and organizing cultural, educational and leisure activities;

e) the **interaction** principle allows us to test out opportunities for informal, spontaneous forms of communication as well as checking for the presence of suitable environments for diversity and variety, as is the case of waterfront linked with historic centres, home to a range of diverse ethnic groups, or neighbourhoods close to large ports, traditionally areas which excel in the ways of trade, transfer and the most lively sort of multicultural community;

f) the **multisectorality** principle highlights the importance of a multifaceted, non-homogenous environment, comprising a combination of living accommodation, manufacturing and commercial businesses, high quality cultural activities and folklore. A dynamic, synergetic environment capable of bridging the development of both technique and art, production and housing, businesses and leisure;

g) and lastly, I want add a further principle, the most important, a systemic principle, the most action-oriented. It's the **perturbation** principle that provides us with a tool to stimulate the "creative milieu" of urban waterfronts, their latent energy required to produce a disturbance within that context and the resultant imbalance between the current situation and a vision for the future, through positive tension experienced by fluid city's inhabitants, moving them to be proactive and overcome the marginal role the area has been assigned. This sort of latent energy is often found in declined waterfront areas where marginalization has produced a certain social unity and widespread discontent generates positive tension, ripe to be guided in the right direction.

The seven principles described above contribute to the achievement of the key development factors: competitiveness, cohesion, innovation and conservation. The following figure shows how and how much each principle contributes to the achievement of the urban development.

The capacity of the Fluid City to pursue simultaneously the principles of competitiveness and cohesion and to ensure the paradigms of innovation and conservation requires a new governance of urban and peri-urban coastal areas. The **Diagram n.8** shows the metamorphosis of waterfront governance following the Fluid City paradigm.

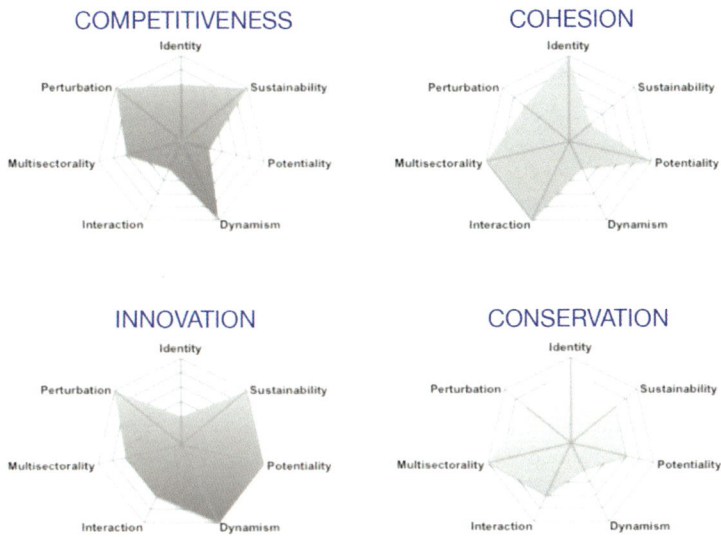

The relationships between port and city will move from **conflict management and separation** of powers in which each actor speaks its own language and states a specified range, towards a permanent integration between the waterfront subjects which would enable any actor to act in a **common ground** and to express themselves within a new dialogue aimed at a permanent interaction between port and city, between land and sea, between places and flows.

Act on the waterfront as a common ground means use a more interactive approach and produces integrated projects able to win the several challenges offered by the urban coastal areas: environmental issues, global competition, urban regeneration, community empowerment and local economy.

FOUR WATERFRONT RELATIONSHIPS

The Fluid City Paradigm is not only a theoretical framework but it's also a projectual devices for reimagining the relationships between water and city. To set up more fertile waterfront regeneration tools we have identified four main relationships between port and city in order to adapt consequential actions towards a greater fluid integration of the Augmented Cities.

The **liquid relationship** is characterized by the prevalence of a coastal identity represented by a landscape where the coastal nature is the mainstream of the waterfront: low interaction between sea and city.

The **fluid relationship** is associated with sailing, cultural and leisure facilities and accommodation: the fluid waterfront is immersed and intertwined with the urban structure, characterised by marinas and cultural and leisure services, and strictly connected to the city. The functions provided for this section relate to the boating, recreational and cultural activities capable of being an integrated interface between city and port: low pressure of the city on the waterfront. **Berlin** is becoming a vibrant fluid city by re-cycling the post-industrial district, like RAW-Gelände (a 7,000 sq m area with a heated pool, beer garden, sun deck, sandy beach and indoor concert venue), in urban lidos where a whole community, young and old, is laying claim to its comfortable loungers, augmenting attractiveness of entire district.

Third variant is the **porous relationship**, namely an area for cruise-ships and passengers, enjoying close ties with the city and transport system, including facilities and buildings along the wharf to encourage the opening of the urban front onto the sea. This type of port is characterised by a large porous area in permanent transformation that acts as a link between the port activities dedicated to passengers and new cultural, residential and commercial activities related to the quality of the waterfront. It manifests a high degree of interaction between the port and city. The porous area between water and city is one in which the fluid metabolism of city finds its design declination through the use of resilient devices and blue infrastructures that not only make more permeable the relationship between cities and coast, but which provide new experiences depending on the amount of water in the dry season or the rainy season, even during severe flooding due to climate change. From the first and most famous experiences of Water Plaza **Rotterdam** is going to improve new projects for permeable areas that allow to define a new urban landscape changing with the water. **New York**, as already mentioned, is becoming a real fluid city realising water permeable parks and floodable spaces, up to the great project by Biarke Ingels for Manhattan to contrast with porous spaces the raise of the Hudson River.

Fourth variant foresees a **rigid relationship**, inaccessible to the public and thus enabling the harbour to work to full capacity: the "port machine" able to guarantee security and safety: high pressure on the city caused by the productive activities.

These four variants are useful to define the depth of the relations between port and city, and contribute to recognise the prevalence of urban or port uses or a dynamic mix of both. Identifying these variants will be useful to lead the choice of specific planning or design tools.

Waterfronts' diversity has to be managed as urban transformer capable of intercepting the tangible and intangible energies crossing along large-scale networks, transposing them into the urban context and translating them into resources for the local development, thus providing vital sustenance to the whole city.

The augmented cities of the future will increasingly take spatial and social form of fluid cities and communities capable of leading the changing relationship between city and port, water and land, urban and human metabolisms towards a renewed alliance and a fertile dialogue.

LIVING WITH WATER

01. The Boston Harbor Association, City of Boston, Boston Redevelopment Authority, and Boston Society of Architects have launched "**Boston Living with Water**", an international call for design solutions envisioning a more resilient, more sustainable, and more beautiful Boston adapted for end-of-the-century climate conditions and rising sea levels. The competition seeks leading planners, designers, and thinkers to help the City of Boston and area businesses and residents to develop and apply new concepts and strategies, including "Living with Water" design principles, to increase the City's sustainability and climate change resiliency. The main topics of the contest are:

a) Design for resilience implies adapting to or bouncing back from a disturbance quickly. Resilient planning and design incorporates redundancy and anticipates change over time.

b) Create double-duty solutions to afford protection in times of need and provide for other uses when idle realizing multiple benefits and maximizing economic, ecologic, and cultural gain.

c) Strengthen community resilience, able to maintain and enhance the cultural identity that defines a city through resiliency networks and social support systems. Strategies that strengthen social resilience can both cost less and provide meaningful benefits to participants.

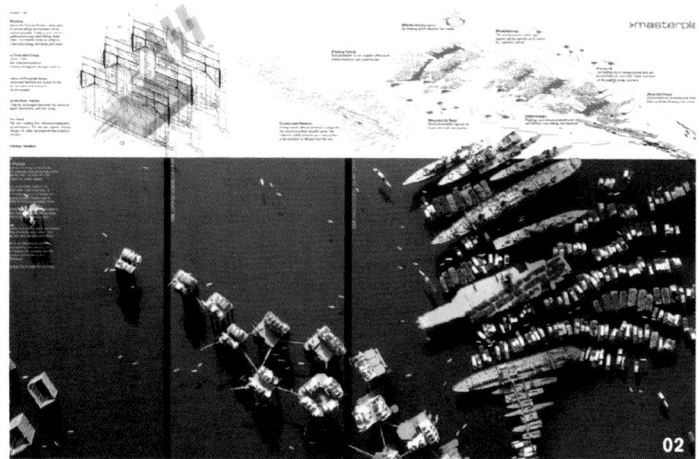

02. Floating City 2030: Thames Estuary Aquatic Urbanism for recycling ships and marine structures, by Anthony Lau, Bartlett School of Architecture, London (2008). With the pressure of increasing population and urbanisation, cities have not choice but to build on flood plains or in low lying areas. One side consequence of humanity's rapid expansion in (arguably) global warming, resulting in rising sea levels and increasingly extreme weather. This conflict between expansion and climatic change threatens coastal cities around the world. One tenth of the world's population live in coastal cities, most of which are low-lying coastal populations in poorer developing nations. Even a 1m sea level rise will result in a widespread economic and social disaster. The future of human habitation and expansion is to adapt to living on water. Every year, hundreds of ships and other floating structures are scrapped. This proposal gives new life to decommissioned ships and oil platforms by converting them into hybrid homes adapted for aquatic living. The Thames Estuary is chosen as the site for aquatic urban expansion, and will be an alternative solution to the current plans to build 120,000 new homes on flood plains in the Thames Gateway. The regeneration of the riverside through the reuse of dockyards, river transport and reverting to a natural hydrology of flood plains will bring nature and life back to the River Thames. Sustainability through the reuse of marine structures and reducing energy and waste will be a high priority when living on the water. By utilising the flooded landscape, a floating city of offshore communities, mobile infrastructure and aquatic transport will allow the city to reconfigure through fluid urban planning. Wave, tidal and wind energy will be ideal for this offshore city and the inhabitants will live alongside the natural cycles of nature and the rhythms of the river and tides. Most modern floating architecture involves new-build modular systems for mass production. Although this may be the most efficient for space planning, it often lacks character. The multitude of hull shapes and sizes can inspire unique and inventive designs. The proposal aims to express the beautiful forms and internal steel structures of hulls. The hulls serve as nautical reminders of the ship's past and our previous closeness to water, which we will now embrace once again. This strategy for creating a self sufficient floating city by reusing ships and marine structures can also be applied to island nations such as the Maldives. Over 80% of its 1,200 islands are around 1 m above sea level. With sea levels rising around 0.9 cm a year, the Maldives could become uninhabitable within 100 years. Its 360,000 citizens would be forced to adapt and they could become the first floating nation.

03. Hammarby sjöstad is an urban development project directly south of Stockholm's South Island. This is no doubt the most referenced and visited spot among Scandinavian examples of implemented eco-friendly urban developments. The original plan of Hammarby was to develop the former industrial area to an ecological sports arena and athlete's village – the aspiration was to develop this area for the Olympics 2012. When the bid was won by London the plans were changed and instead the Stockholm municipality – together with a number of construction companies – decided to make this the first Ecocity district in Stockholm for the first millennium. One new feature of the Ecodistrict, which has won international recognition, was to integrate several infrasystems in the planning from the very beginning: technical infrastructure, mobility and communication infrastructure, building infrastructure and to some extent green-blue infrastructure. Another strong feature is the system of interdisciplinary planning of physical flows of energy, water and waste. The overall goal is that the environmental impact caused by emissions from Hammarby shall be 50 % lower than the corresponding level for housing areas from the early 1990s.To obtain these goals, integrated planning, innovative solutions and new technologies have been necessary. Objectives for 2015: a) Transport & mobility: 80% of travelling by using public transport; 25% electric / biogas vehicles; b) Energy: energy consumption of buildings of 50 kWh/m2 out of which 15 kWh/m2 for

electricity; 100% RES; usage of 80% energy from waste; biogas production from sludge; all waste and waste water coming from the inhabitants will be recycled and returned to the area in the form of renewable energy; c) Water: 60% reduction of water consumption/person; d) Waste: 90% reduction of landfill waste and 40% reduction of all waste produced; reclaim of one half of the nitrogen and water, and about 95% of phosphorus, in the waste in order to use these as fertilizer for agricultural activities in the area; e) Urban planning: inner-city architecture; 10000 apartments for 25000 inhabitants living and working in Hammarby; f) Social: citizen involvement; attractive and sustainable places to live and work. The project runs until 2016, and today more than half of the project area is complete. Further, when the project is complete, Hammarby Sjostad aims to achieve a compact urban community served by a fast train, pedestrian and bicycle-friendly environment in order to reduce the need for cars. All of these steps, taken together, will ensure a more attractive, healthier and more environmentally- friendly community.

04-05. Rotterdam is going to experiment the city as a fluid organism of several flows. As infrastructure and citizens become more technologically-enabled than ever before, this concept of urban flow becomes easier to measure. The immense amount of data generated in cities can offer us an improved understanding of how everything from water to waste to people to cargo moves around. Which is exactly what. FABRIC and James Corner Field Operations have done as part of their new show at the International Architecture Biennale Rotterdam. Called "Flow Animations", the team describes the project as the first visualization of Rotterdam's metabolism, creating nine videos that show the movement of Rotterdam's urban landscape. Exploring the impact of the river Rhine on Rotterdam, the **Water Flow** video looks at the importance of the Rhine's fresh water supplies for Rotterdam. A city is reliant on its flow of goods, providing citizens, business and

other urban services with the essentials they need to operate. Rotterdam is certainly a noteworthy example of this, being home to the largest port in Europe. The **Goods Flow** video explains how the 220 million tonnes of goods that pass through Rotterdam's port move through the city and beyond, using waterways, roads, railways, and other ports. Interestingly, though Rotterdam handles twice as much volume as nearby Antwerp's port, it only employs 17% more people in port-related industry. The **Energy Flow** video looks at the energy mix in the Netherlands, along with the energy efficiency of Rotterdam. Fossil fuel supplies in the Netherlands are being depleted, and renewable energy is yet to make up for this. Additionally, all companies in the Port of Rotterdam combined lose an amount of heat equal to twice the amount of the total capacity of all planned and existing wind turbines in the North Sea.

The city shows, today even more clearly, its evolution towards an increasingly complex and comprehensive system, a self-aware mix of varied functions (including rural dimension and landscape patterns) and towards a product made of local collective skills. In the new, extended, networked and multipolar metapolis – a true urban planet –, the city's plural nature is increasingly rebelling against single functions and a mono-centric approach.

9. RETICULAR

THE TRANSCONNECTED SOCIETY
Metropolitan super-organisms and territorial archipelagos

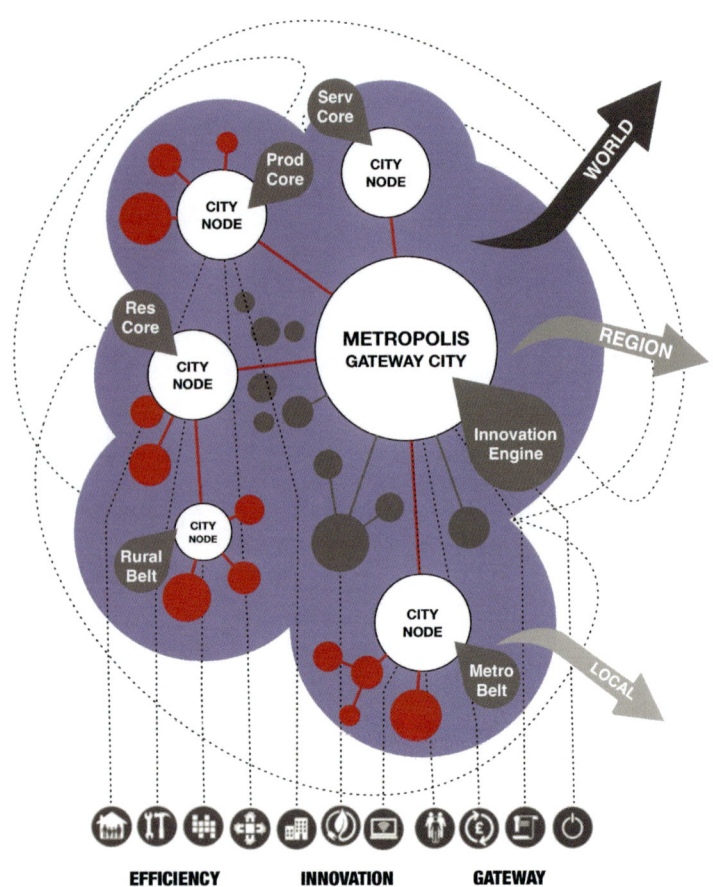

CITY AS EXCHANGE HUB

The studies of Enrico Moretti (2012) about new geographies of jobs in metropolitan regions show how, starting from the U.S. but with increasing evidence in Europe, the functional relationships and mobility flows between cities no longer follow a traditional gravity model. The more adequate representation of metropolitan relations – or post-metropolitan to quote Soja (2000) – is a dense network of nodes and lines that draw complex and multiple relations, not referable to an univocal client-server relationship, but more similar to the cloud computing.

We live in a hyper-metropolitan world where cities follow polycentric and reticular shapes, are gathering fluid mode, constantly change drawing variable geometries producing polymorphic geographies. The metropolitan regions generate new complex metabolisms involving the cities as a specialised hubs in permanent innovation and redefinition of their life cycles.

During the last decade several European countries have revised their territorial metropolitan model towards a non-gravitational one, such as France, Germany and Poland. Italy too is revising its metropolitan framework based on a more actual view of territorial relations, whose purpose is to build established national lines that go beyond the traditional local and global settlement, at the territorial level and as regards government contexts, hubs and networks. The overall picture emerging from governmental documents is divided into three territorial situations:

a) the **spatial-based productive platforms** consisting of emerging districts that have been able to diversify and gain access to major international circuits, implementing successfully competitive production systems. However, such districts are still in need for public policies to increase accessibility to large networks and enhance connections between local and global spheres, thus allowing them to take root in the context-territory preventing unsustainable unbalances between poles of competitiveness and local territories;

b) the **regional hub cities** consisting of those city-regions that have the ability to act as switches between major European and international

flows and the local sphere, naturally predisposed to act as innovative environments, thus likely to influence and promote changes in the existing social and productive systems. Cities are therefore interpreted and presented as drivers of competitiveness, energy transformers that run through global networks, diffusers and fertilizers benefiting their context in a necessary logic of spatial equity, as fundamental component of territorial cohesion. "Exchange cities, revolving platforms, concentration and redistribution places", as Le Corbusier defined them in 1963. These hub-territories, together with the network of middle-weight cities whose task is to promote cohesion between various development experiences at different speeds, are the cornerstone of Italy's future settlement. Here, the transformation match is being played, towards new economy, technological innovation, knowledge and experience economy; and there is more: it is precisely here that public investments for attractiveness will have to allocate their efforts;
c) the **connecting infrastructures** viewed as effective combination of the various flow networks that will have to ensure the adequate release of digital services and knowledge, the fundamental prerequisite and added value of contemporary economy, other than facilitating communications between people and goods.

Contemporary city is increasingly characterized by its relation with railway, marine, air and land infrastructures and related logistic equipment, but also by its connections with broadband digital networks integrated with education and research centres. Contemporary city is a network of networks.

HORIZON 2020: INFRASTRUCTURE-TERRITORY-CITY

In Europe, the contribution to defining reference perspectives for the investment management and spatial planning in the 2020 horizon on "infrastructure-territory-city" integrated system is based on a combination of three systems: a) the high added value urban contexts focusing on competitiveness and attractiveness of the territory through national and transnational strategic territorial platforms; b) the strategic networks of relationships, not just infrastructures but also the functional and organizational interdependencies between urban territories aimed at strengthening the cohesion patterns; c) the switch poles fundamental for the spatial and functional armature of metropolitan cities and second-tier urban areas designed to connect the global and local sphere adopting a new collaborative approach.

The consequential action will be developed within a specific decision-making environment relying on multi-level governance, which inevitably leads to inter-scalar action. Resources and local interests that make up the identified platforms are coupled with resources and national and regional interests. In this way, they contribute to a development scenario characterized by the local sphere owing to its important role for national competitiveness. On the other hand, supralocal resources and interests are oriented to local resources and interests, thus contributing to pinpointing interest and investments.

The vision of the future is supposed to be able to address the following issues: a) outlining action strategies to return to territories, identities and local vocations those connecting qualities that can promote clustering or distrectualization logics, permanently fuelling the national and transnational infrastructure flows; b) definition of the key elements of an effective strategic territorialisation, which does not understand territory as an abstract entity onto which to project socio-economic decisions, but looks at it as a project producer, selector of instances, a voice to be heard and capital to be turned into value; c) identification of the intrinsic and contextual characteristics of the instruments which should implement tangible projects and, consequently, delivering significant results.

The overall objective to be pursued for recovery and reactivation of growth productive factors and the social progress ones is to shift from an Europe based on urban hubs (namely the few Metropolitan European Growth Areas) to a networked Europe whose development goal is the interconnection between hubs and the setting up of an armature of second-tier cities (the Functional Urban Areas), leading to the territorial excellence-based Europe (driven by cultural, infrastructural and landscape resources).

METROPOLITAN CITY AS SUPER-ORGANISM

The city shows, today even more clearly, its evolution towards an increasingly complex and comprehensive system, a self-aware mix of varied functions (including rural dimension and landscape patterns) and towards a product made of local collective skills. In the new, extended, networked and multipolar metapolis (Ascher, 2009)– a true urban planet – the city's plural nature is increasingly rebelling against single functions and a mono-centric approach.

The spatially concentrated city, divided through parts and functions, is being replaced by "archipelagos cities", divided into epicentres, and by the "city-network", complex hub of networked and open urban armatures intertwined with as many global and local networks. The outcome runs the risk of an identity loss brought about by the constant search for models produced by third parties generating a fuzzy meta-urban entity instead of a multiple and rich identity.

One of the responses to contemporary cities' anomia, in their progressive loss of a complex identity in favour of micro-specific identities – often in conflict –, is the creative application of the principles of vocation and polycentricity, in order to ensure a greater variety and liveliness within the urban fabric. Housing, work, production, culture and leisure must all be linked with one another in time and space, not only to reduce the travel time, to save energy, reduce pollution, to allow time for socializing, but more generally to rethink the parts of the city and the cities within the same functional region as a system of interacting communities. Rethinking the development model shall also focus on the metaphors that have accompanied it. The eco-system has set the example as regards the need for interaction among all development actors. But biology teaches us that the ecosystem is effective as long as the competition between organisms does not become fierce (owing to a sharp contraction of resources or overpopulation for example), which would eventually lead to the system's self-destruction. The diagram below shows the situation of most of the existing relations between the core and the belts: all active flows related to economies and services go to the center that no longer has the resources to fulfill them effectively. The result is a hyper-attractiveness, a frustrating distribution of

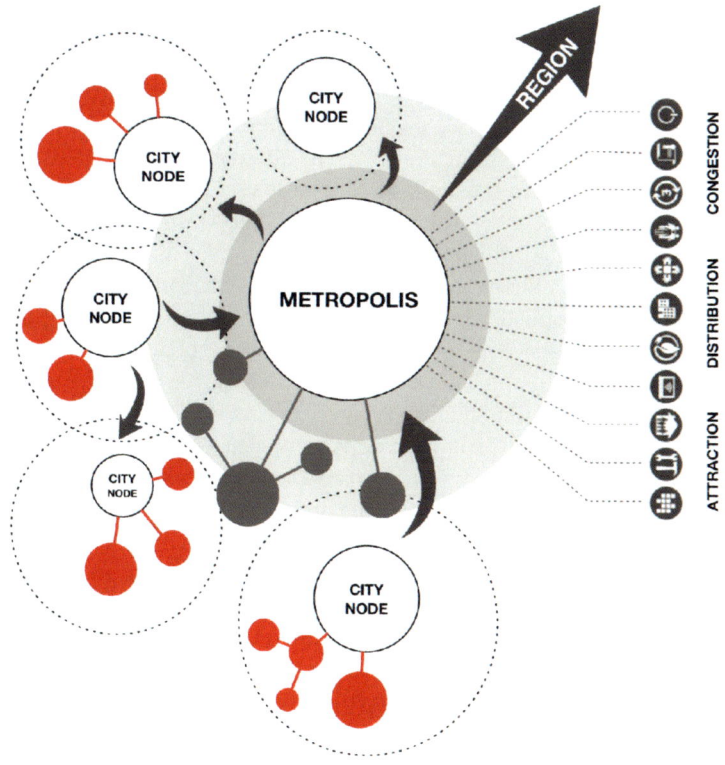

flows, and above all a constant congestion that generates discomfort and degradation rather than facilitate economies of scale for which the metropolitan relation was initiated. We have to redefine the metropolitan relation with a more collaborative mode.

Which is why we ought to shift to the "super-organism" metaphor, i.e., the amount of individuals organized in societies where everyone plays a clearly defined role and — as components of a perfect mechanism — move in unison contributing to the incremental development of the organism. In the **Diagram n. 9** we show new metropolitan relationships as a super-organism based on innovation and cooperation. The **Metropolitan Super-organism** is above all a polycentric system, a human settlement of networks and hubs, offering numerous opportunities, diversifying by identities and resources of places. The core city, therefore, is a **gateway city** that acts as a urban engine to redistribute the flows from it towards others nodes. So the super-organism is a system of systems of **specialized city nodes** that act as service core, residential core, rural belt or productive belt, with a more effective distribution of function regarding gateways, innovation and efficiency. The Metropolitan Super-organism through its distribution of coordinated territorial specializations is most effective in transcalating dialogue with global, regional and local levels. Its non-gravitational organization allows it to strengthen the competitive role of all his components in keeping with the holistic approach of the Augmented City. In this way **cooperation** replaces gravitation and the system back into balance even with a reduced amount of resources available, ready to generate new drawing on the potential of an open and distributed system. Open source against hierarchy.

To achieve these objectives, urban policies are needed at the local level because it allows functional integration without forcing anybody to move to large urban centres, and allows the continuous implementation of appropriate projects capable of preventing urban decay, uprooting or standardizations that too often characterize urban belt systems. Policies will have to take into account the needs of the different communities inhabiting in the urban armatures of the future, avoiding to uncritically privilege the main hubs, producing new poly-centres instead, and to focus only on the mono-thematic economic capital. The social, cultural and spatial capitals shall be enhanced towards the city-networks (Cattan, 2007).

NETWORKED POLYCENTRISM AND TERRITORIAL ARCHIPELAGOS

Networked polycentrism might be able to act not only as a functional integrator (of housing and services), producing positive effects on the urban and spatial planning, but also as a catalyst of new settlement cores, especially based on the cultural and identity matrix. Strengthening the identity, however, is not enough since the city lives and evolves only as a global/local network hub of mutual connections and synergies, where cities and local systems compete in a supra-local scenario to turn into development driving forces (Albrechts and Mandelbaum, 2005). The ability to use and target the competitive advantage linked with the presence of a varied local milieux not only characterised by functional and localization conditions (the traditional Atlantic and Central European polycentric systems), but increasingly generated by cultural identity or quality landscape (the new polycentric systems of the Mediterranean and Latin arc) is synonymous with successful strategy in the increasingly fierce urban competition.

These urban patterns act as "Territorial Archipelagos", drawing from their own stories and apparent marginalization, are now able to offer significant hubs to connect to the global networks (through thematic networks for example) and other smaller local entities, otherwise excluded by larger networks. The territorial archipelago is an urban and rural settlement system connected by landscape, productive, and mobility infrastructures that act as connective interfaces.

The connective system of the territorial archipelago consists of a perimeter belt of landscape made around urban areas with different ecosystem functions: agricultural/ productive, river corridor, re-naturalisation fields, sport facilities, slow mobility, etc. (Carta, 2017). The archipelago-park becomes the connective tissue of urban islands and their framework of resilience. The territorial archipelago doesn't act as a single organism like the previous super-organism, but uses the power of its reticular relations sharing identities, roles and hierarchies.

Several Mediterranean polycentric systems, such as Andalusia and Murcia (Spain), Provence and Languedoc-Roussillon (France), the network of green cities in Murgia and Madonie and the World Heritage List historical centres of Val di Noto (Italy) have been experimenting, for years now, the local rooting of green infrastructure and digital infostructures networks, cultural and slow-living armatures, open technological skills as well as innovation within local administrations. This self-management ability of the local domain empowers the minor local actors to grasp the competitive advantages offered by local networked systems in the new European challenge.

In the same direction acts the EU project called **URMA** (Urban-Rural Partnership in Metropolitan Areas) aimed to improving urban-rural cooperation and contributing to territorial cohesion. The URMA project promotes urban-rural partnerships as a tool to strengthen the potential for generation and transfer of innovation in European metropolitan areas and their surrounding hinterlands. Urban-rural partnerships can be characterised by some relevant spatial aspects: a) at the small scale: inner-metropolitan area of cooperation between metropolitan core and its periurban areas (e.g. Florence metropolitan area); b) at the medium-scale: inner-metropolitan region cooperation between urban areas and rural areas. This also includes predominantly rural areas with a polycentric structure (e.g. Twente-Borne); c) at the large scale: supra-regional cooperation of metropolitan core /area /region with rural hinterland, defined on a more global scale (e.g. Hamburg-Jutland). The urban-rural cooperation is based on equal footing, respect and recognition of mutual interdependence between urban and rural actors. The cooperation will fail in the long term if it will be dominated by hierarchical structures and stereotypes. Urban-rural partnerships should enable peripheral and economically weak areas to participate in growth and innovation. Metropolitan areas as engines of development have responsibility to initiate projects from which less favoured areas would profit. Solidarity in the context of URMA is based on finding the balance between competition and support. Support in this context can be understood as an exchange of know-how, good practices and innovative solutions.

However, not all cities respond in the same manner to the spatial networking stimulus. Not so much because there are urban milieux with different degrees of potential, but especially because not all of them rely on the adequate social capital to establish relational networks able to turn them into collective actors on the supra-local stage. The passive understanding of urban identity as individual local rooting and sense of belonging to the local environment, exclusively intended as heritage to be protected and preserved, is being gradually replaced by an active and creative concept, according to which resources and cultural services are sources of competitive advantages and identity becomes an active link between the various actors endeavouring to include hub-cities in the global networks' wider game. Committing to the construction of the European hub-cities does not mean acting within a process which is exclusively led from outside – even if significantly promoted by European policies – but taking active steps in a context that needs a significant political cooperation: metropolitan super-organisms and territoriali archipelagos will be the big players in reticular Europe. They could generate networks of different voluntary cooperation among cities enlivened by talents, values and roles that a new reticular planning approach will have to be able to extract from urban identities and human cultures.

TOWARDS HYPER-METROPOLIS

01. The **Territorial Archipelago** diagram shows the richness of fluxes and relations in an urban and rural settlement system connected by local identities, landscapes and productive infrastructures. The archipelago doesn't act as a single organism like the super-organism, but use the power of its reticular relations sharing identities, roles and hierarchies to reshape hyper-metropolitan patterns. Polycentrism, resilience and inclusion are the key connecting factors of the rural-urban settlements that compose the archipelago (Carta, 2017).

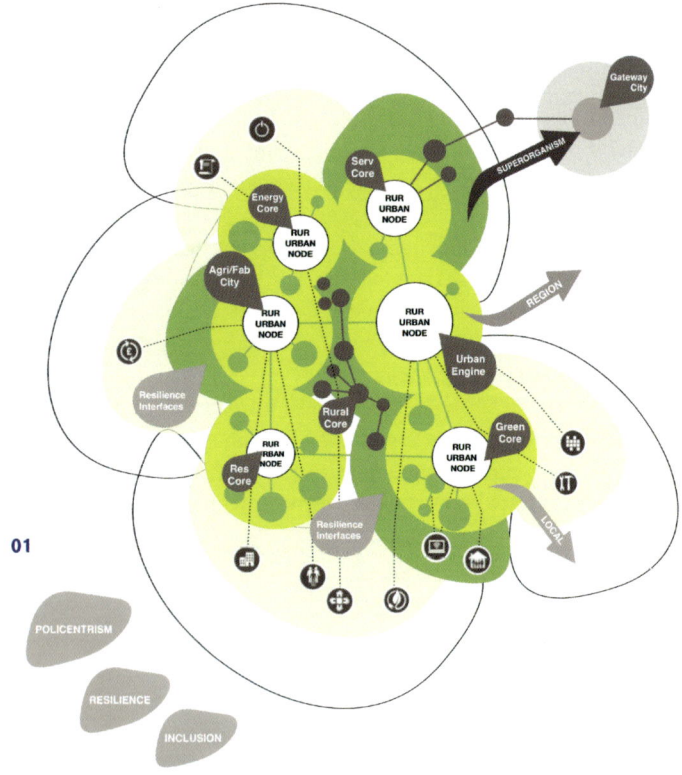

LES PROJETS DE POLES MÉTROPOLITAINS

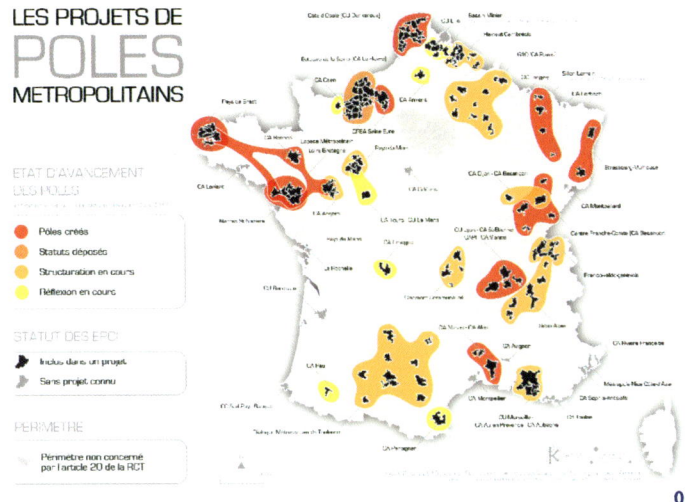

02. The **French Pôle Métropolitain** is a mixed syndicate of intercommunal municipalities with their own tax established by the law about local government reform, and intended to foster cooperation between large towns near located in large urban complexes or development corridors. The law about modernization of territorial public action and affirmation of metropolises (called MAPAM law) has made some changes on demographic thresholds and possible status of metropolitan centers. The Pôle Métropolitain is a public institution established by agreement between the Établissements Publics de Coopération Intercommunale (EPCI) with their own tax, to govern metropolitan interest on economic development, promotion of innovation, research, higher education and culture, space management by coordinating the territorial coherence schemes. The Pôle acts also on infrastructure development and transport services, to promote a model of sustainable development of metropolitan center and improve the competitiveness and attractiveness of its territory, as well as the development of the infra-departmental territory and sub-regional levels.

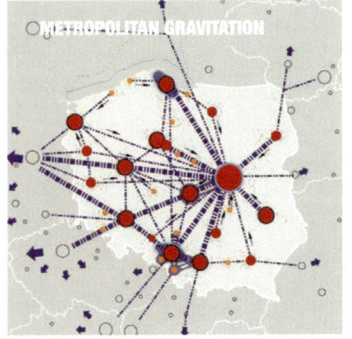
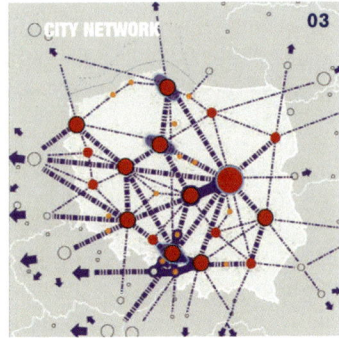
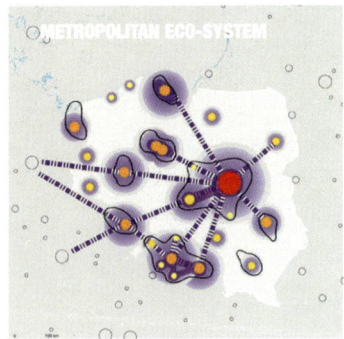
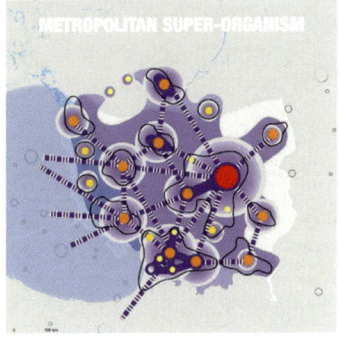

03. Diagrams of the different types of **metropolitan relationships**. Top row: the evolution from traditional gravitational model to the city network. Bottom row: the difference between the metropolitan eco-system and the metropolitan super-organism. The last is a polycentric system, a human settlement of networks and hubs, able to offer several opportunities, diversifying by identities and resources of places. The super-organism is therefore a "system of system" of specialized city nodes that act as a stronger organism.

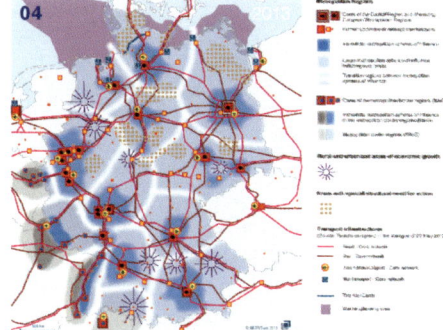

04. The overall objective of **URMA Project** is to promote urban-rural partnerships as a tool to strengthen the potential for innovation in European metropolitan areas. Therefore, sub-objectives are: a) Interregional exchange of experiences on urban-rural cooperation/partnerships; b) Identification of different types of urban-rural partnerships as well as regional innovation systems, taking into account Partner's good practices; c) Improving the effectiveness of regional and local policies in the field of innovation generation within urban-rural partnerships. This will enable the establishment of a regional, national and European policy agenda for a sustainable development of metropolitan areas. Moreover, it will result in lasting and balanced positive effects on the competitiveness of metropolitan areas, also in global terms. The key advantage to this approach is that urban and rural areas will benefit on equal terms and that cities will not gain competitiveness at the expense of rural areas and vice-versa. The step taken with the initiation of the Demonstration Project of Spatial Planning for crossborder functional regions (**MORO güV**) and, above all, with the establishment of the Cross-Border Metropolitan Regions Initiative (IMeG) was essential for the discourse regarding cross-border metropolitan regions (CBMRs) in Germany. An important basis for the later work of the IMeG had already been created in the first MORO phase. This basis strengthened the network, provided orientation for the network's strategic direction, and served positioning on the national and European level. Today the Federal Government assesses the path taken with the two Demonstration Projects as a success. This view is shared by the project partners as the Demonstration Project has generally created a good and systematic basis on which the cross-border metropolitan regions can continue to build in the future as well.

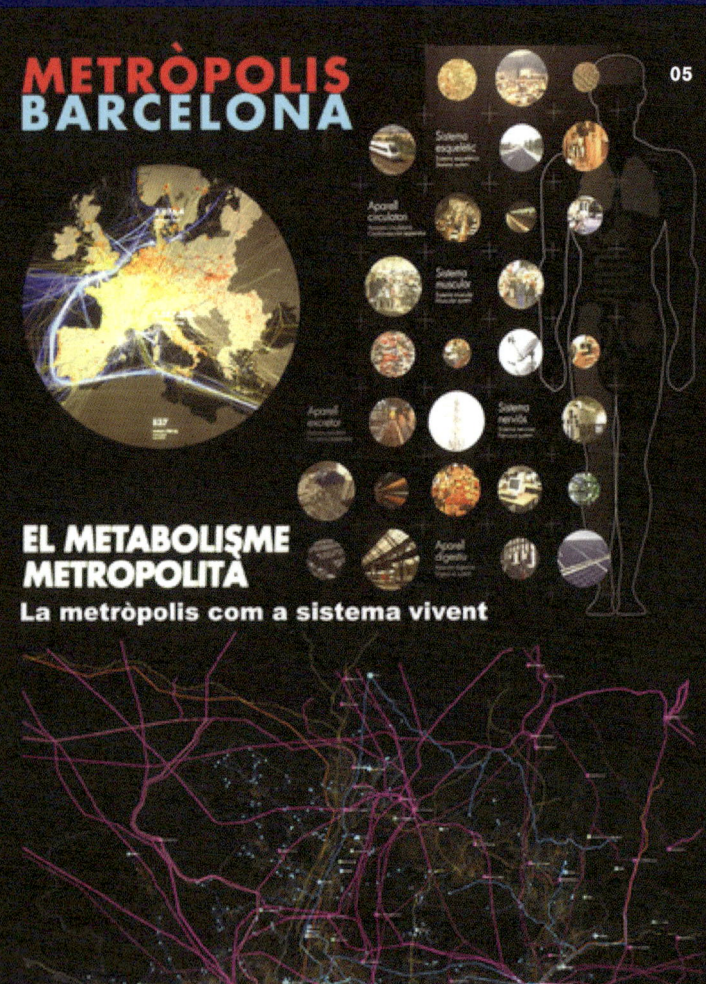

05. The Area Metropolitana de Barcelona has realized the exhibition **Metròpolis Barcelona**, an initiative that shows the reality of this metropolitan territory in all fields. The exhibition complements the process of defining the new Metropolitan Urban Plan-PDU. Cities of the metropolitan area of Barcelona share policies, infrastructures, labour relations and markets, education and culture, housing, health, security, mobility, energy and supplies, etc. Civic life has become metropolitan. Its geographic situation and urban culture, its valuable history, the compactness of its growth have generated the powerful dynamics experienced since the late nineteenth and throughout the twentieth century. The transformations of the last forty years, in its urban spaces as well as in economic and residential activities, have placed it as a significant city in the European scene. One of the most important paradigms on which will be based the future of the metropolitan area will be the metropolitan metabolism. The city is a physical space, but above all it is a functional space, where daily life develops and is maintained thanks to the constant flow of food, raw materials, energy, water and people. The exhibition shows a dynamic explanation of the metropolis: the metropolitan reality changes over time. While the physical form of a city is the result of a slow but dynamic construction, the behaviour patterns of its inhabitants in public space vary according to the time of day or the month of the year. But all this generates manufactured products, waste and emissions.

The **Metròpolis Barcelona** will reimagine the metabolism based on circular economy and landscape matrix: ecology, leisure, creativity and production will be the component of the new metropolitan archipelago. In the new reticular Barcelona streets, squares and parks can re-naturalise themselves and connect with metropolitan parks and with those agricultural and natural areas that we still keep. In this direction acts the plan based around the idea of superblocks (*superilles*), mini neighbourhoods around which traffic will flow, and in which spaces will be repurposed to "fill our city with life", as its tagline says. Barcelona's new plan consists of creating big superilles through a series of gradual interventions that will repurpose existing infrastructure, starting with traffic management through to changing road signs and bus routes. Superblocks will be smaller than neighbourhoods, but bigger than actual blocks. This will first be applied to Eixample neighbourhood and others like Sant Martí and Poblenou, which largely follow the same grid pattern and which allow to experiment the integration of housing and production (the Fab City we mentioned in Chapter 4).

The age of experience of strategic planning financed by public funds has replaced the age of innocence of the first deliberate preparations; the driving force of heresy has been replaced by the quiet force of dogma.
Augmented Cities need real and effective strategic processes, incremental and adaptive, that not only refuse the traditional and ineffective top-down approach, but that will not yield to the comfortable bottom-up tactics.

10. STRATEGIC

THE HYPER-STRATEGIC PLANNING

Incremental and adaptive planning processes

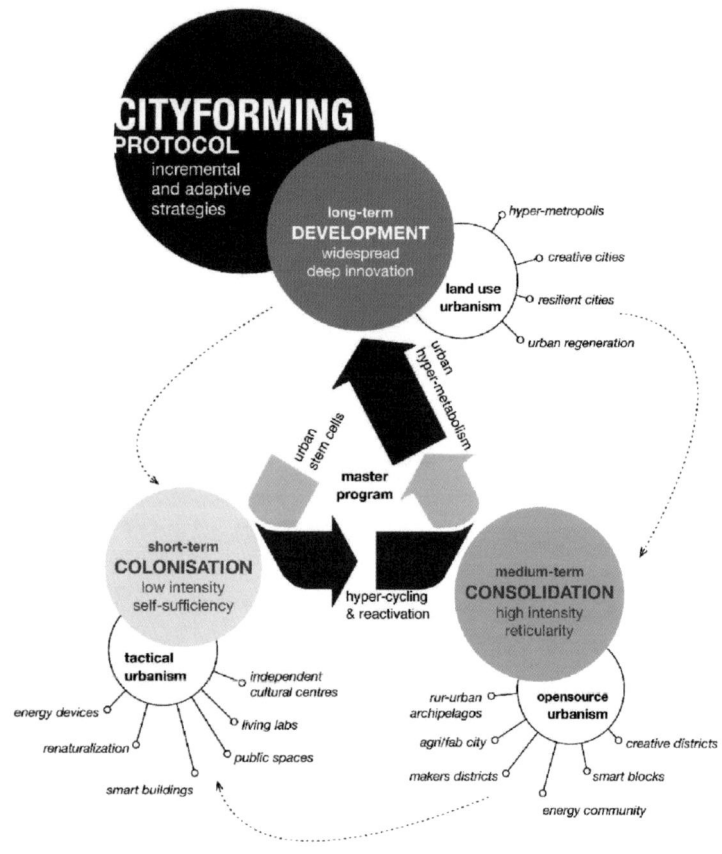

HOLISTIC, INCREMENTAL AND ADAPTIVE APPROACH

Augmented City isn't only a new paradigm, but it needs to be implemented for being the habitat of the Neo-Anthropocene. It needs a new strategic approach, more effective and less rhetorical. The challenge is set up **hyper-strategic plans** for territories undergoing longstanding development crisis — we are in the tenth year of the symptoms and the pathologies are in their 20s. The task of incremental adaptive plans reminds us of the rigorous assessment of the interaction between five converging and interacting domains, able to act to integrate the three major issues of sustainability: economic (for profit), social (for people) and ecological (for planet). In the next figure each of domains is investigate as producer of specific set of products:

a) the primacy of the **spatial domain** (territorial and environmental) requires the establishment of urban quality as growth engine, providing stimulus for rural areas as social connectors, contributing to the active conservation of cultural and landscape resources and to energy efficiency as prerequisite for environmental sustainability and social cohesion within a new welfare state. The strategic plan, abandoning the comfortable and safe procedural approach, is faced with the responsibility of finding concrete answers to current problems of people's lives, which in turn becomes the best certification of the effectiveness of its procedures;

b) the role of the **management domain** is fundamental to define processes and tools for agreements between actors, aiming at co-planning and at achieving and implementing the objectives, as well as identifying assessment systems. The dynamism of cities and communities urges the plan to establish appropriate "sensors of change" able to react in a timely manner to re-orientate strategies and reprocess actions according to contextual changes;

c) the stimulus provided by the **economic domain** does not only identify the necessary capital to provide resources for feasibility, but above all creates added value from the interaction of different capitals (financial, human, social and territorial), reassembling patterns, increasing the mass but especially orienting the correct destination. The appropriate use of different capitals within a single direction allows raising the social return on investments in terms of aggregate productivity, the lack of which today is one of the most serious diseases of development;

d) the **regulatory domain** ensures the definition of rules aimed at protecting choices over time or in case of leadership changes, it is fundamental to provide guarantees to joint actions of the actors and to define the relationships between the different implementation tools, which are essential for the effectiveness of the strategic plan, not only aiming at an interaction of subjects, but above all of tools and skills;

e) the opportunities of the **communicative domain**, as a structural process *in itinere* instead of *ex post*, aim at promoting the covenant of community among the various subjects for strengthening the vision and share it for a collective empowerment towards the project of future supported by the plan. In the Augmented City the communicative dimension of plans and projects does not present itself as a superstructure; on the contrary, it profoundly affects the generative phase of the plan, fuelling the ability to build and strengthen the relational system that supports it.

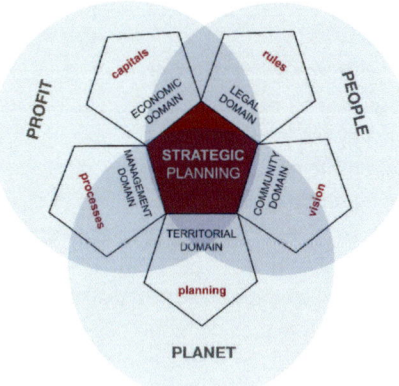

FIVE STRATEGIC DRIVING PIVOTS

Which actions are to be implemented to ensure the strategic plans' effectiveness, the strengths on which to bank on, the critical issues to be addressed and the threats to be avoided? Five driving pivots may be identified as cleaver planning aims to be not only more effective and sustainable, but especially a significant driving force:

a) the participation pivot urges us to avoid the "meetings" rhetoric when it comes to decision-making, leaving the easy navigation of forums aside to go through the turbulent deep sea of true partnership, shared responsibility and co-planning. The distinction between different forms of listening to the demand, sharing goals and negotiating the implementation ought to be rigorously ensured, recognizing the different values and the associated operational modes;

b) the critical mass pivot requires us to make our choices within a competitive framework assessing the scope, other than the quality, of the territorial dimension establishing the driving system that will nurture the plan's implementation, understanding the across-scale modality not as wide tension but as a complex intention to act within metropolitan and regional platforms;

c) the relational pivot requires strategic plans to be more than a driving force and a stimulus, but to represent proper "distribution chains" of their effects, fuelling the local relational system and, if necessary, establishing dedicated cross-fertilisation networks within their contexts thus increasing the micro-social networks' power;

d) the leadership pivot focuses on the need to lead and provide regulations for the many processes started by the strategic plan, avoiding uncritical and rhetorical shift from government to governance but rather experimenting innovative management practices, turning them into sound leadership, authoritarian regulation if necessary and cooperation practices, as much empathetic as they are necessary;

e) finally, the clear view pivot, which ought to govern the entire planning process, filling its visions with content, turning them into maps guiding the various actors involved, especially the exogenous or supra-local ones. The engine's quality is no longer enough, as the efficiency of transmission and the ability of the driver: above all, taking the adequate direction in order not to conflict with the neighbouring contexts is essential.

The above described pivots strengthen the ethical dimension of strategic planning laying its foundations: the social capital, consisting of the human, intellectual, cognitive, relational, creative and political capitals, is fundamental to heal the pathologies and returning strategic planning to its non-dissipative and generative origins.

The lack of social capital in terms of a shared culture that limits opportunistic behaviour by fostering cooperation is one of the critical issues to be tackled when it comes to dealing with Southern Europe. Re-building the social capital requires the implementation of an open process characterised by accountability and awareness of the role (the necessary empowerment that must be coupled with the strategic plans), able to act on all layers of society, strengthening the community tissue and the role of the élites, returning dreams to younger generation and ambitions to the older.
In the last few years, regional planning policies regarding development and urban regeneration in disadvantaged areas have implemented interventions that characterised by the "dead frog aporia". Their irresolvable contradiction is actually comparable to the well-known Eighteenth-century experiment carried out by Luigi Galvani on frogs, whose thighs kicked, when crossed by an electric current, as if in life. The territories in a state of decay, run-down cities wounded by post-industrial closures, entrepreneurs suffering the economic crisis have attempted to defeat death by injecting European or National funds as power energy into diseased organs – even necrotic – or attracting international events, setting urban enterprise zones, signing district contracts, establishing urban regeneration companies and so on. The effect was often tragically identical to the frog experiment: the induced driving force had

simulated life, often mistaken – with hope or illusion – with neighbourhoods blossom, tissues regeneration, recovery of the economic system or even with the city renaissance. In fact, as soon as the energy input was interrupted, as frogs legs returned hopelessly death, the regenerated areas become desolate decaying places again, run-down spaces, urban living simulacra. Especially in the Mediterranean Europe, the illusion of frogs resurrection has to be necessarily avoided, replacing the energy produced by political capital – based on patronage systems and welfare state – with the vital energy of social capital based on quality and projects generation. A new policy capable of reactivating and lead the development of the South, as well as more effective instruments, will need to find a new ruling class that knows how to generate visions, implementing actions and manage global networks.

NO MORE MASTERPLAN: THE CITYFORMING PROTOCOL

In Europe the season of urban regeneration (started in Nineties with the Urban Program) has produced important effects both in the review of the design devices and in the rethinking of the settlement forms and their spatial and human relations. But it cannot be hid the emergence of certain diseases that often have anaesthetised, when not cancelled, the regenerative effects envisaged. The transition, while it has increased the use of urban regeneration processes from the bottom, at the same time extended the epidemic of failures derived from a top-down approach. The critical issues of hierarchical urban regeneration cannot be solved by revising the procedures for participation, improving design devices or innovating implementation processes, but it overturned the view. In the Augmented City the regeneration of urban areas characterised by marginalisation and decline, by the disposal of buildings and infrastructure, and by the functional underuse or weak activity of cycles (mobility, water, waste) needs a real and effective process that must take an approach that not only refuses the traditional and ineffective top-down strategy, but that will not yield to the, rhetorical and superficially comforting, tactical bottom-up.

From the Augmented Cities comes a shout: **no more masterplan**! Now we need a hyper-strategic approach, ethically circular, programmatically incremental, procedurally recursive and projectually flexible, rather than a closed and simultaneous strategy. The traditional masterplan, inflexible, instantaneous and almost unchanging in its implementation – ineffective in areas that cannot enjoy the destination of significant public or private resources (now almost disappeared in transition European cities) – we have to replace a "masterprogram" knowingly temporised and adaptive, capable of composing a comprehensive vision by implementing piecemeal, capable of timely and temporary action but that have the generative force of a new future that knows how to turn on autopoietic and self-sufficient processes.

In times of crisis of development models, of the transition of settlement patterns and of the reduction of public resources, the sustainability of urban metamorphosis should be implemented through a regenerative process that proceeds by successive cycles, driven by an overall vision, but capable to adapt to the concrete outcomes of the implementation process.

A hyper-strategic urban regeneration must create itself the conditions for success to feed the next steps, it should produce a portion of the value on which to trigger the subsequent investment; it must generate the oxygen that fuels the urban atmosphere from which stand to the new life housing, productive, commercial and cultural relations that will regenerate the area.

We need a sort of "terraforming" applied to the city: an incremental process designed to make re-living by a new community the abandoned or declining area, acting through the connective skill of its territorial components still active – creating new ones, changing their composition or facilitating interactions – in such a way as to make it capable of supporting a new ecosystem. Terraforming was a NASA's protocol for colonising other planets developed with the collaboration of James

Lovelock. He defined life as an autopoietic system with feedback loops: life is generated from cells or from more complex organs that interact within a larger organism, or individuals acting within a social context of interdependencies. Before to implement the urban regeneration of declining areas and the new colonisation of abandoned urban space, we need to activate – or reactivate – the pre-condition of human development, the starting condition for the settlement of new human life. Therefore I call **Cityforming**© **Protocol** this self-regenerating process, a planning protocol – a system of rules and actions not a standard or a model – able to reactivate by stages the stationary metabolism of an area, starting from its latent regenerative components, enabling multiple cycles, increasing intensity to create a new urban sustainable ecosystem over time. The strategic Cityforming acts for incremental and adaptive steps required to produce partial results that become the foundation of the next generative phase.

The **Cityforming**, progressing through the stages of creative colonisation, community consolidation and sustainable development, produces first the necessary "urban oxygen" for the formation of an appropriate ecosystem able, then, to generate a new active metabolism that reactivates inactive cycles, reconnects the broken ones or that actives new ones, stimulating new settlements more adapted to the identity and ambition of transition places.

The conceptual model (**Diagram n.10**) shows the sequence of the three phases with their characteristics and projectual devices. In the first short-term phase of **creative colonisation** some functions are localised in order to act as reserves of oxygen for the formation of the new atmosphere. There are new functions or recovery of buildings or spaces that can be called "stem cells" because, although grafted through planning action, they have not dissimilar features and functions from existing tissue. These urban stem cells act as a new urbanity activators – in different forms through which we express the city –

and can be ecological areas of naturalisation, plug-in energy devices, low-cost smart buildings, living labs, redevelopment of public spaces, independent cultural centres, reactivation of small trade of proximity, etc. Colonisation, also, is implemented through the removal of some infrastructural or environmental detractors that reduce the vitality of the area to facilitate the reconnection of ecological networks for the reconstitution of the environmental network. The regeneration colonies are characterised by a high self-sufficiency and generated by their ability to be energetically autonomous through a massive use of renewable sources, their ability to produce sufficient profitability to support the maintenance costs, their ability to activate forms of widespread partnership for management. The colonies must also have a strong recognisability with respect to the context, because, although low-intensity processing, they serve as landmarks of the transformation, act as witnesses to the reputation of the district, operate as urban marketing agents. The prevailing paradigm that is used at this stage is that of the *Tactical Urbanism* with a three-year time horizon within which the next step to be activated. In the US, for example, there are several initiatives of incremental and adaptive experience of urban regeneration, such as the Better Block Urban Design, founded in **Dallas** Oak Cliff by Jason Roberts and Andrew Howard, and the experienced in **Memphis**, **St. Louis**, **New York** and **Boston** as an exemplary tool to produce new temporary visions of a space to show the transformative potential to create a safe walkable, lively and creative neighbourhood. But urban tactics or the variegated forms of Pop-up City and DIY regeneration are almost always self-consistent, content to redevelop the space of their action, no escaping the risk of infertility from the structural effects and the risk of their premature exhaustion. The colonisation of Cityforming, however, presupposes a subsequent local roots, creates the conditions for triggering a chain reaction that strengthens the effects.

The **community consolidation** is the second medium-term phase. It affects the new ecosystem being formed by grafting some more valuable and powerful features from the point of view of the generation of profits and economic values. This step is financially supported by the increase of land value and attractiveness of the area. Ecological and smart blocks, makers districts and energy communities, green factories and attractors for new rur-urban archipelagos or infrastructural gateway, micro-productive districts for digital manufacturing act through a hyper-cycling process that activates several cycles in order to achieve a sufficient supply of attractive and productive functions. The consolidation also acts through the reactivation of latent resources already present in the area and which have been stimulated and positively perturbed by the step of colonisation. The consolidation phase acts more for networks that for nodes and loses a bit of his self-sufficiency and autonomy, often starting to use the local resources – the material ones but more often those intangible – to take root and grow, also starting a process of camouflage with the context that reinforces its presence. Are often the existing residents who help new users attracted to the colony in the integration process. At this stage some tactics or some actions of "third landscape" *à la Gilles Clement* from the previous phase are involved in an *Opensource Urbanism* process that modifies them, mixing with the local intelligences, integrating with urban acupuncture actions, so as to transform them into strategies to extend in depth their reactivation effects of urban cycles. In this phase, with a five-year horizon, the initial flows produced by the attractiveness of users is replaced with the stability of new residents that contribute to grow demand for services and to strengthen the care for places, including agreements and pacts.

Lastly, the **sustainable development** is the third and long-term phase with a horizon at least ten years, in which the new metabolism of the area is put into operation to generate new urban values. At this stage, following the metamorphosis produced by the first two phases, can be drawn up a masterprogram of the whole area based on the new identity of the place. It would be made more fertile by the success of the previous stages, being able to tap into a greater investment multiplier effect, able to support the infrastructural investments required for completing the transformation of the area. In this phase, the master-program makes sense since it acts in a time of change and in a more advanced stage where the decision-makers and the community can best verify the soundness of the development vision. It is not, therefore, a comprehensive masterplan that assumes in advance the conditions for its implementation or which intercepts economic and entrepreneurial resources already given, but is a flexible land use plan acting on new urban ecosystem and that is specified as the changed conditions of the re-colonised and consolidated area. In this step it generates the necessary deep innovation capable of allowing the construction of eco-cities, creative districts, new metropolitan municipalities, urban development projects, regional parks connecting urban and rural dimension and new integrated platforms within new development scenarios and complex territorial equipments allowed the completion of the Cityforming.

CITYFORMING	**MASTERPLAN**
is incremental	is instantaneous
is open	is closed
plans by steps	acts by steps
is strategic	is regulative
is dialogic	is conformative
enables urban tactis	defines land uses
activates scenarios	anticipates scenarios
produces new metabolism	acts by separate layers
acts by programs	acts by projects
generates community	settles populations

The **Cityforming** approach doesn't implement a predefined view for temporal excerpts. It refuses a preliminary top-down planning process that requires huge financial resources for its full implementation and the activation of a high land income or real estate revenue for the realisation of all the infrastructures.

The Cityforming generates, however, a program of actions, tactics, controlled testing and re-appropriations that are composing and defining in function of the partial results, based on the consolidation of new roles in the urban area, based on values and expectations that are generated by new inhabitants, new services and forms of cooperation, by the tax facilities and by new urban economies generated in the first two phases. So the third phase can stand on the new urban/human ecosystem solidified by the first two. The Cityforming constantly working within the dimensions of the project and the process, active actions within a predicted scenario the effects of which will set up the specification and definition, consolidating the trend scenario or helping to form a new programmatic scenario.
The process of Cityforming, therefore, not only has to set incrementally processing and reactivation actions of latent resources and interrupted cycles, but it acts as an antidote to the gentrification often related to urban regeneration. Colonisation, indeed, precisely because of its transformative low intensity and for its generative stem function on new spatial and social tissues, does not induce an instantaneous transformation that eradicates the local identity for the benefit of an external attractiveness. But colonising actions act as catalysts of the local identity resources, working on the palimpsest rather than on his conforming superfluity.

In the Augmented City the **Cityforming Protocol** is the most adequate enabling and generative tool for planning and design, for augmenting urban/human values we need. It is not just an urban design and planning strategy or an innovation in urban policies, but acts as a powerful disruptor of territorial organisms in anaesthetised metabolism, in reduced or in declining vital energy. It does not act by entering external energy, which could not keep active for a long time the compromise metabolism, but takes care of the internal tissues still present vital factors, redials the latent ecological resources, reactivates the resilient social networks, revives the anaesthetised manufactures to generate the indispensable basis of territorial and social capital on which it can take root the fruitful seed of the sustainable regeneration project in the Neo-Anthropocene.

CITYFORMING PROCESS

01.a

01. The **High Line in New York** is an exemplary case of Cityforming: in the colonization phase were local residents who have reactivated the old railway line, now inherent in their views of identity, through a up-cycling project that has transformed it into connection public space. Then the consolidation was carried through the intervention of property developers who have acted to extend the effects of the renewed attractiveness of the area and to root the results, enabling the upgrading of buildings and other places to bring the residence, professional activities, trade and to introduce services to tourism. Finally, the development phase has recently started with the creation of the new Whitney Museum designed by Renzo Piano that marks the transformation of the Meatpacking District in a neighborhood of creativity and innovation. Not surprisingly Samsung has opened a representative office here, Google his New York-based headquarter and Apple one of his store, but also a proliferation of urban gardens and the Center for Social Innovation is always filled with more new business. The completion of the development phase consists of the master plan for the realization of the Hudson Yard Development, the largest private urban regeneration operation in New York after the Rockefeller Center:

158 hectares of commercial space, office and residential (half of which public spaces) and cultural centers, among which the extraordinary Culture Shed, designed by Diller Scofidio + Renfro. The High Line, with its colonizer effect, first of all has completely redesigned the socio-cultural map of New York, then redefining also the map of the talents, creativity and innovation, as well as real estate that generates profits for the management and maintenance. The incremental and generative action of Cityforming prevented that there was a glut in the market and spaces not leaving any more opportunities to the inhabitants indeed expelling them, as happened in the Seventies in SoHo

and Eighties in Chelsea. In fact it was precisely the action of colonization of the local residents, joined together in the Friends of the High Line, prevented the planned real estate speculation and replaced it with care spaces, the infrastructure re-naturalization, the safety of places: actions that have consolidated the social fabric and the human capital on which they are established interventions with greater added value.

02. The **Cityforming Protocol** was experimented for the first time in 2014 for drawing a Masterprogram for the Palermo South Waterfront able to activate a package of policy, regulatory amendments and design actions to implement district regeneration and other urban management guidance applicable to the adoption of local shoreline strategic-driven and recycle-based plan. In 2016 the protocol was used in Open Taranto Competition for the regeneration of "Città Vecchia" (the historic district). **Cityforming Taranto** was the proposal by Mario Cucinella Architects, Maurizio Carta, Patrizia Di Monte, Luigi Oliva, Studio De Vita & Schulze Architetti, Tms Engineering Srl, and others. The proposal has won the special mention "for public involvement in the process of transformation and for establishing a solid incremental process for its implementation". The project, called "Taranto respira" (Taranto breathes) is implemented through three incremental phases, timed, which allowed to define an action program self-sustainable, low cost and with intensive effects. Each action creates the necessary conditions for the implementation of the next, in a real own metabolic process that limits the use of considerable external resources. The first phase is the "creative colonization" (3 years), in which they are localized certain initial functions that serve as activators of context, or are removed some infrastructure or environmental detractors which reduce the quality of the area; the second phase is the "collaborative consolidation" (5 years), in which the new ecosystem in formation are grafted some functions finest and most powerful of the point of view of the generation of profits and values, cost incurred by the increase in value and attractiveness of the area; the third phase is the "sustainable development" (10 years), through the realization of an overall masterplan based on the new identity of the place, made more fertile by the success of the previous stages, with a multiplier of the investment of greater strength, and thus able to support the major investment required for the complete transformation of the area. The urban regeneration project, based on the reactivation of the life cycles of the area and on the hyper-cycling of functions, was processed through three stages that have allowed us to verify the real effects on territory, population and decision-makers. The first phase of startup regards the activation of new low-cost activities, the second phase of rooting concerns the residential system and the quality of public space, the third phase of legacy is the one that allows to reactivate all urban cycles to return Taranto old district creative, intelligent and resilient, consists of several integrated and interacting functions. Strategic actions generate a new urban/rural grid composed of specialization nodes and connectors of material and immaterial flows. The process generates informal actions, collaborative contracts and a vibrant creative improvement district policy based on the new digital manufacturing, on social innovation and on education facilities.

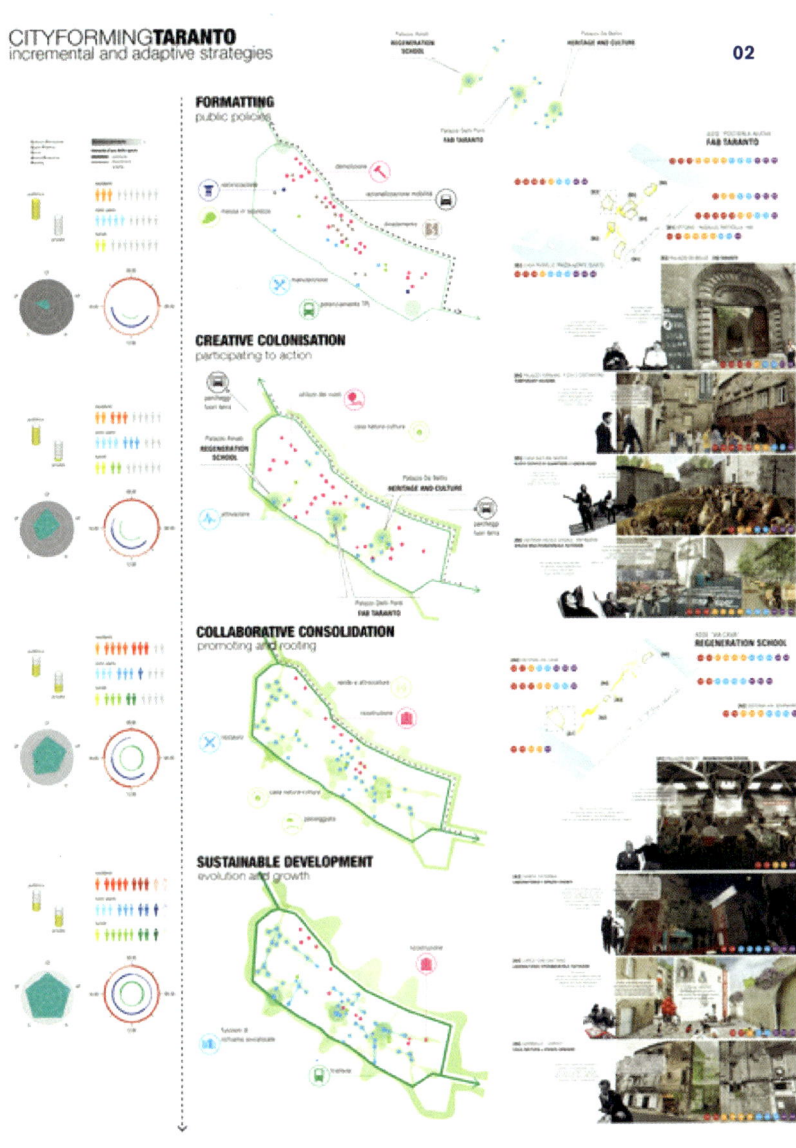

03.a

03. NYC (Steady) State, a project by Terreform (Center for Advanced Urban Research). This large-scale inquiry seeks to answer the question: can New York City become self-sufficient within its political boundaries? Intended to be an alternative masterplan for the city's future, this study investigates the possibility for urban self-reliance in such areas as food, energy, waste, water, air supply and quality, manufacture, employment, culture, health, and transport. The predicate of the study lies both in questions of the limits of sustainability and in a response to the failures of democratic autonomy in an increasingly globalized economy. The study aims to produce not simply a dramatic new plan for the future of New York but to compile an inventory of best practices that are relevant to cities around the world. For New York City to successfully transition into self-sufficiency, a number of enabling morphological transformations must occur. One of which is the "figure-ground switch", in which nineteenth century blocks see their built mass migrate into the space of the street, freeing the block interior for the inscription of agriculture and other public uses. Terreform has devised three discrete master plans for New

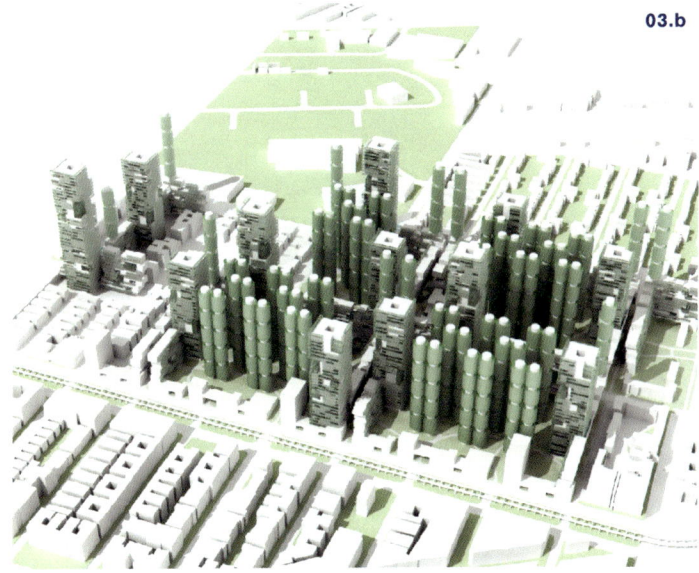

York City. Each plan builds on a spatial inventory that identified key locations throughout the city where conventional and advanced food production could be sited. The diagram in the center shows the production capacitiy of each borough in Master Plan A. Where there is surplus (Staten Island & Queens), food is redistributed to make up for the gap between population and production capacity of the other boroughs (Bronx, Brooklyn & Manhattan).

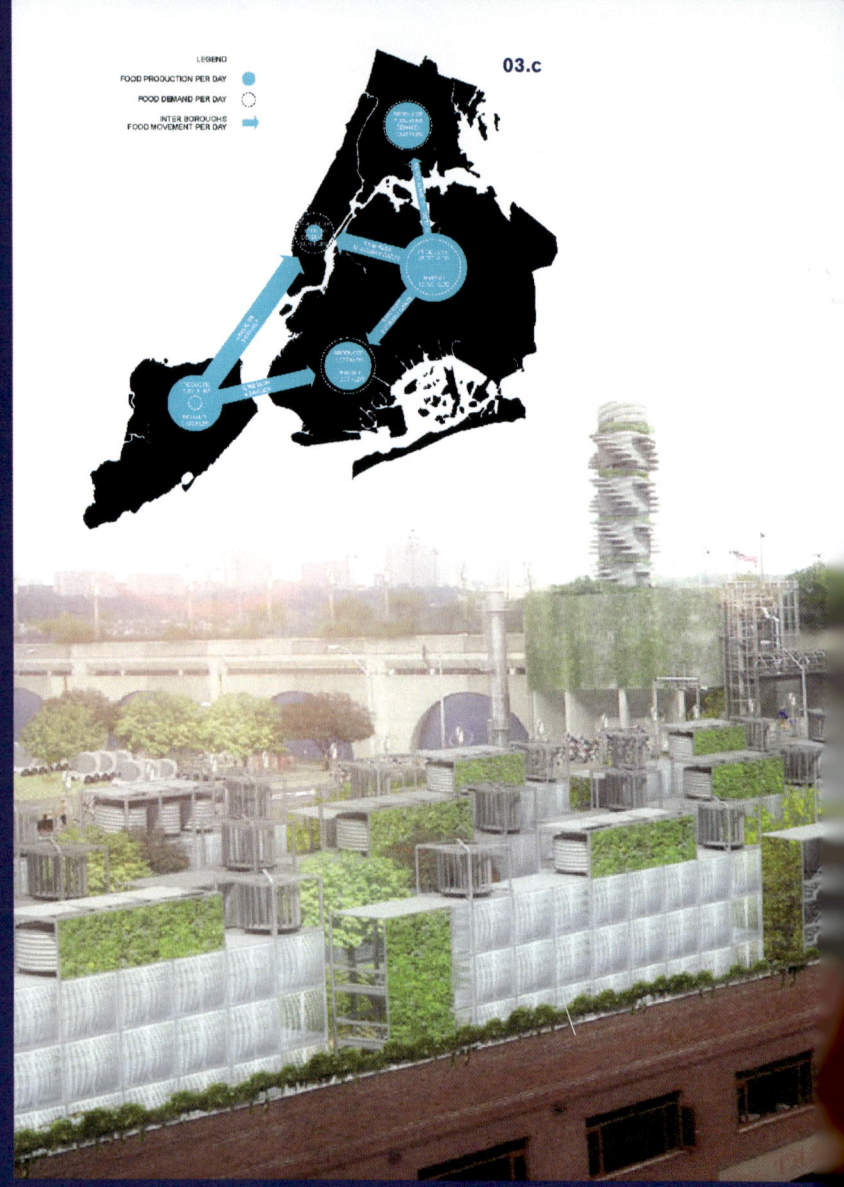

03.d

REFERENCES

— Albrechts, L. and Mandelbaum, S.J. eds. (2005), *The Network Society: A New Context for Planning.* London: Routledge.

— Alexander, C. and Reno, J., eds. (2012), *Economies of Recycling: Global Transformations of Materials, Values and Social Relations.* London: Zedbooks.

— Anderson, C. (2012), Makers: *The New Industrial Revolution.* New York: Crown Business.

— Aravena, A. and Iacobelli, A. (2012), *Elemental: Incremental Housing and Participatory Design Manual.* Ostfildern: Hatje Cantz Verlag.

— Ascher, F. (2009), *L'âge des métapoles.* Paris: Edition de l'Aube.

— Berger, A. (2007), *Drosscape: Wasting Land in Urban America.* Princeton: Princeton Architectural Press.

— Brynjolfsson, E., McAfee, A. (2014), *The Second Machine Age. Work, Progress and Prosperity in a Time of Brilliant Technologies*. New York: W.W. Norton & C.

— Bullard, R.D. ed. (2007), *Growing Smarter: Achieving Livable Communities, Environmental Justice, and Regional Equity.* Cambridge: Mit Press.

— Campbell, K. (2011), Massive Small. *The Operating Programme for Smart Urbanism.* London: Urban Exchange.

— Campbell, T. (2012), *Beyond Smart Cities: How Cities Network, Learn and Innovate.* New York: Routledge.

— Carta, M. (2007), *Creative City. Innovations, Dynamics, Actions.* Barcelona-Trento: ListLab.

— Carta, M. (2014a), *Reimagining Urbanism. Creative, Smart and Green Cities for the Changing Times*. Barcelona-Trento: ListLab.

— Carta, M. (2014b), Smart Planning and Intelligent Cities: A New Cambrian Explosion. Riva Sanseverino E., Riva Sanseverino R., Vaccaro V., Zizzo G. (eds.) *Smart Rules for Smart Cities. Managing Efficient Cities in Euro-Mediterranean Countries.* Springer.

— Carta, M. (2016), Re-cyclical Urbanism. A planning agenda for circular metamorphosis. in Carta, M., Lino, B. and Ronsivalle, D. eds., *Re-cyclical Urbanism.* Barcelona-Trento: ListLab.

— Carta, M. (2017), Planning for the Rur-Urban Anthropocene, in Schröder, J., Carta, M., Ferretti, M, Lino, B., eds., *Territories. Rural-urban Strategies.* Berlin: Jovis.

— Carta, M. and Lino, B. eds. (2015), *Urban Hyper-Metabolism.* Roma: Aracne.

— Carta, M. and Ronsivalle, D. eds (2016), *The Fluid City Paradigm.* Berlin: Springer.

— Carta, M., Lino, B., Ronsivalle, D. eds. (2016), *Re-cyclical Urbanism*. Barcelona-Trento: ListLab.

— Castells, M. (2012), *Networks of Outrage and Hope: Social Movements in the Internet Age.* Cambridge: Polity Press.

— Chapain, C., et al. (2010), *Creative clusters and innovation. Putting creativity on the map.* London: NESTA.

— Ciorra, P., Marini, S. eds. (2011), *Re-cycle.* Milano: Electa.

— Cattan, N. ed. (2007), *Cities and Networks in Europe. A Critical Approach of Polycentrism.* Montrouge: John Libbey Eurotext.

— Coyle, S.J. (2011), *Sustainable and Resilient Communities: A Comprehensive Action Plan for Towns, Cities, and Regions.* Hoboken: John Wiley and Sons.

— Dolgin, A. (2009), *The Economics of Symbolic Exchange.* Berlin: Springer.

— Ellen MacArthur Foundation (2012), *Towards the Circular Economy: Economic and business rationale for an accelerated transition.* EMF.

— European Climate Foundation (2010) *Roadmap 2050. A practical guide to a prosperous, low-carbon Europe.* Den Haag: ECF.

— European Commission-Regional Policy (2011), *Cities of Tomorrow. Challenges, Visions, Ways Forward.* Brussels: European Commission.

— European Commission, Directorate-General for Research and Innovation (2012), *Global Europe 2050.* Luxembourg: Publications Office of the European Union.

— Fabian, L., Munarin, S., eds. (2017), *Re-cycle Itali Atlante.* Siracusa: LetteraVentidue.

— Ferrão, P. and Fernández, J.E. (2013), *Sustainable Urban Metabolism.* Cambridge: MIT Press.

— Florida, R. and Tinagli, I. (2004), *Europe in the Creative Age.* London: Demos.

— Gallagher, J. (2013), *Revolution Detroit: Strategies for Urban Reinvention.* Detroit: Wayne State University Press.

— Gausa, M. (2009), *Multi-Barcellona, Hiper-Catalunya. Estrategias para una nueva Geo-urbanidad.* Trento-Barcelona: List

— Graham, S. and Marvin, S. (2001), *Splintering Urbanism: Networked Infrastructures, Technological Mobilities.* London: Routledge.

— Greenfield, A. (2013), A*gainst the smart city.* New York: Do Projects.

— Guallart, V. (2012), *The Self-Sufficient City: Internet has changed our lives but it hasn't changed our cities, yet.* Barcelona: Actar.

— Hajer, M., Dassen, T. (2014), *Smart about Cities. Visualing the Challenge for 21st Century.* Rotterdam: nai010 publishers.

— Hatzelhoffer, L., Humboldt, K., Lobeck, M., Wiegandt, C. (2012), *Smart City in Practice. Converting Innovative Ideas into Reality.* Berlin: Jovis.

— Hebert, F. par (2015), *Villes en transition. L'expérience partagée des Ecocités.* Marseille: Parenthèses.

— IAAC (2012), City Sense. *Shaping our Environment with Real-Time Data.* Barcelona: Actar.

— Ibanez, D. and Katsikis, N. (2014), *New Geographies 06 - Grounding Metabolism.* Cambridge: Harvard University Press.

— Jackson, T. (2009), *Prosperity without Growth. Economics for a Finite Planet.* New York: Earthscan.

— Johnson, S. (2010), *Where Good Ideas Come From: The Natural History of Innovation.* New York: Riverhead Books.

— Kaletsky, A. (2010), *Capitalism 4.0: The Birth of a New Economy in the Aftermath of Crisis.* New York: Perseus.

— KPMG (2016), *Innovation through craft: opportunities for growth*. London: Kpmg.

— Kunzmann, K.R. (2014), Smart Cities: A New Paradigm of Urban Development. *Crios*, n.7.

— Landry, C. (2007), *The Art of City Making*. London: Earthscan.

— Markopoulou A. (2014) In[form]ation - *Architecture of Data & Code.* Barcelona: IaaC bits, 1.3.3.

— Marsh, J. ed. (2013), *The Human Smart Cities Cookbook.* Peripheria Project.

— McCann, E. and Ward K. eds. (2011), *Mobile Urbanism. Cities and Policymaking in the Global Age*. Minneapolis: University of Minnesota Press.

— McDonough, W., Braungart, M. (2013), *The Upcycle: Beyond Sustainability--Designing for Abundance.* New York: Melcher.

— Moretti, E. (2012), *The New Geography of Jobs.* New York: Houghton Mifflin Harcourt.

— Mostafavi, M. and Doherty, G. eds (2010), *Ecological Urbanism.* Baden: Lars Müller Publishers.

— Offenhuber, D. and Ratti, C., eds. (2014), *Decoding the City: How Big Data Can Change Urbanism.* Zurich: Birkhäuser Verlag Gmbh.

— Otto-Zimmermann, K. ed. (2011), *Resilient Cities. Cities and Adaptation to Climate Change - Proceedings of the Global Forum 2010.* Heidelberg: Springer-Verlag GmbH.

— Owen, D. (2009), *Green Metropolis, Why Living Smaller, Living Closer, and Driving Less Are the Keys to Sustainability.* New York: Riverhead Books.

— Patel, M., Sotsky, J. et al. (2013), *The Emergence of Civic Tech: Investments in a Growing Field.* Miami: Knight Foundation.

— Ratti, C. (2015), *Open Source Architecture.* London: Thames & Hudson.

— Ratti, C. and Sassen, S. (2009), Le megacittà iperconnesse. *Aspenia*, 44.

— Ratti, C., Claudel, M. (2016), *The City of Tomorrow: Sensors, Networks, Hackers, and the Future of Urban Life.* Yale: Yale University Press.

— Reed, C., Lister, N.-M. (2014), *Projective Ecologies.* Barcelona: Actar.

— Ricci, M. (2012), *New Paradigms.* Trento-Barcelona: ListLab.

— Ridley, M. (2010), *The Rational Optimist: How Prosperity Evolves.* New York: Harper.

— Ronsivalle, D. (2016), The fluid city experience: an update, in Carta, M., Ronsivalle, D., eds., *The Fluid City Paradigm. Waterfront Regeneration as an Urban Renewal Strategy.* Zurich Springer.

— Rodin, J. (2014), *The Resilience Dividend: Being Strong in a World Where Things Go Wrong.* New York: PublicAffairs.

— Rockström, J and Klum, M. (2015), *Big World, Small Planet: Abundance within Planetary Boundaries.* Yale: Yale University Press,

— Ryan, B.D. (2014), *Design After Decline: How America Rebuilds Shrinking Cities.* Philadelphia: University of Pennsylvania Press.

— Sassen, S. (2011), Open-Source Urbanism. The New City Reader: *A Newspaper Of Public Space,* n.14, january.

— Schröder, J., Carta, M., Ferretti, M, Lino, B., eds. (2016), *Territories. Rural-urban Strategies.* Berlin: Jovis.

— Sennet, R. (2012), *Together: The Rituals, Pleasures, and Politics of Cooperation.* New Haven: Yale University Press.

— Shepard, M. ed. (2011), *Sentient City. Ubiquitos Computing, Architecture, and the Future of Urban Space.* Cambridge: MIT Press.

— Sijmons, D. (2014), The Urban Metabolism, in Brugmans, G., Strien, J., eds., *Urban by Nature.* Rotterdam: IABR.

— Soja, E.W. (2000), *Postmetropolis. Critical Studies of Cities and Regions.* Oxford: Blackwell.

— Sommariva, E. (2014), *Cr(eat)ing City. Strategies for the resilient city.* Trento-Barcelona: ListLab.

— Storper, M. and Scott, A. J. (2009) Rethinking human capital, creativity and urban growth. *Journal of Economic Geography.* n.9.

— Swilling, M. (2014), Towards Sustainable Urban Infrastructures for the Urban Anthropocene. Allen A., Lampis A. and Swilling M. (eds.), *Untamed Urbanism.* New York: Routledge.

— Terrin, J-J. par (2014), *Villes inondables. Prevention, adaptation, resilience.* Marseille: Parenthèses.

— Townsend A.M. (2013), *Smart Cities: Big Data, Civic Hackers, and the Quest for a New Utopia*, W.W. Norton and Company.

— Varnelis, K. (2014), Eyes That Do Not See: Tracking the Self in the Age of the Data Center. *Harvard Design Magazine.* n. 38.

— Zolli, A. (2013), Resilience: *Why Things Bounce Back.* New York: Simon & Schuster.

— Unesco (2015), *Reshaping Cultural Policies. A Decade Promoting the Diversity of Cultural Expressions for Development.* Paris: Unesco.

— UN (2017), *New Urban Agenda. Resolution adopted by the General Assembly on 23 December 2016.* New York: UN.

AUGMENTED CITY
A paradigm shift

Author
Maurizio Carta

Published by
ListLab
info@listlab.eu
listlab.eu

Art Director & Production
Blacklist Creative, BCN
blacklist-creative.com

ISBN 9788899854201

**Printed and bound
in the European Union**,
July 2017
September 2018 (re-print)
February 2019 (2nd re-print)

series

All rights reserved
© of ListLab edition;
© of the author's texts;
© of the author's images.

No part of this book may be reproduced, stored in a retrieval system, or transmitted in any form or by any means, including electronic, mechanical, photocopying, microfilming, recording or otherwise without written permission from the publisher.

Sales, Marketing & Distribution
distribution@listlab.eu
listlab.eu/en/distributori-promotori-ditributors-promotors/

For more information concerning ListLab's Scientific Boards please visit the webpage:
listlab.eu/en/board-comitati-listlab/

ListLab was established in 2007 and has elaborated on the idea of an international editorial laboratory with a multidisciplinary approach to architecture, planning, arts, photography, and design. **List Group**, found in 2021, aims at creating networks and promoting debates and cultural exchange, but also organize events from which new knowledge about architecture, cities, and landscape can develop. Today, List Group is composed of **ListLab**, the publishing house, **Blacklist**, the graphic design studio, **Instaura**, the informational weblog, and **Us/Them/Yours**, a creative agency that aims at a multimedia approach to information.